FEATURES

AUTUMN 2022 • NUMBER 33

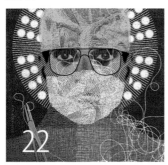

Plough

DEPARTMENTS

WEB EXCLUSIVES

Read these articles at *plough.com/web33*.

Plough
ANOTHER LIFE IS POSSIBLE

EDITOR: Peter Mommsen
SENIOR EDITORS: Maureen Swinger, Sam Hine, Susannah Black Roberts
EDITOR-AT-LARGE: Caitrin Keiper
MANAGING EDITORS: Maria Hine, Dori Moody
BOOKS AND CULTURE EDITOR: Joy Marie Clarkson
POETRY EDITOR: A. M. Juster
DESIGNERS: Rosalind Stevenson, Miriam Burleson
CREATIVE DIRECTOR: Clare Stober
COPY EDITORS: Wilma Mommsen, Priscilla Jensen
FACT CHECKER: Suzanne Quinta
MARKETING DIRECTOR: Trevor Wiser
UK EDITION: Ian Barth
CONTRIBUTING EDITORS: Leah Libresco Sargeant,
Brandon McGinley, Jake Meador
FOUNDING EDITOR: Eberhard Arnold (1883–1935)

Plough Quarterly No. 33: The Vows that Bind
Published by Plough Publishing House, ISBN 978-1-63608-064-2
Copyright © 2022 by Plough Publishing House. All rights reserved.

EDITORIAL OFFICE
151 Bowne Drive
Walden, NY 12586
T: 845.572.3455
info@plough.com

SUBSCRIBER SERVICES
PO Box 8542
Big Sandy, TX 75755
T: 800.521.8011
subscriptions@plough.com

United Kingdom
Brightling Road
Robertsbridge
TN32 5DR
T: +44(0)1580.883.344

Australia
4188 Gwydir Highway
Elsmore, NSW
2360 Australia
T: +61(0)2.6723.2213

Plough Quarterly (ISSN 2372-2584) is published quarterly by
Plough Publishing House, PO Box 398, Walden, NY 12586.
Individual subscription $36 / £24 / €28 per year.
Subscribers outside of the United States and Canada pay in British pounds or euros.
Periodicals postage paid at Walden, NY 12586 and at additional mailing offices.
POSTMASTER: Send address changes to
Plough Quarterly, PO Box 8542, Big Sandy, TX 75755.

Letter on page 108: Reprinted by arrangement with The Heirs to the Estate of Martin
Luther King Jr., c/o Writers House as agent for the proprietor New York, NY. Copyright
© 1957 by Dr. Martin Luther King, Jr. Renewed © 1985 by Coretta Scott King.

Artwork by Tony Abeyta reprinted by permission from Acosta Strong Fine Art Gallery.

ABOUT THE COVER:
A vow is a binding promise, made
with the intention of holding fast.
As an illustration of this we have
a reef knot, an ancient and simple
binding knot commonly used by
sailors. The artwork is part of a
series of knot paintings by British-
Australian artist Brian MacShane.

Readers respond to *Plough*'s Summer 2022 issue, "Hope in Apocalypse." Send contributions to *letters@plough.com*.

LASTING HOPE

On Peter Mommsen's "Hoping for Doomsday": So eye-opening to understand the difference between apocalypse as fear and punishment and apocalypse as unveiling. My spouse and I read this together and found it very helpful in reshaping our views of what's important in a time of war in Ukraine, Covid, etc. I guess I wonder if we're being told to stop worrying about the future and focus simply on the moment we're in? Like plant a tree now, then go meet your Messiah.

Nicole Solomon, Monticello, Georgia

I have found myself, all too often lately, "doomscrolling" through articles on climate change. This article is such an antidote to the fear and anxiety that come from this kind of empty pursuit. Just recently, I started reading through Revelation again. I couldn't quite put my finger on why I would go there given my depressing focus on climate and civilization collapse. Your article exactly articulated why: I'm looking for my true and lasting hope in and through all this. My heart's true cry in hope is in concert with the Spirit and the Bride – "Come Lord Jesus, come!" Our Morning Star signals the end of the night and the start of a new day, that's where my focus needs to be . . . while tending to His garden, even as damaged as it is.

John Geffel, Oregon City, Oregon

LIFE'S NOT SAFE

On Brandon McGinley's "Everything Will Not Be OK": Mr. McGinley didn't mention the Covid plague we're stumbling through. I use the word "stumbling" advisedly, given the shambolic response our various public health, government, and cultural institutions have provided since the arrival of the virus. I believe, though, very much in line with the author, that our current cult of safety has driven us past the edge of what was once considered sane – dare I say adult – behavior. It seems clear to me that this obsession with an unattainable level of assurance in the preservation of our mortal bodies derives immediately from what Alexander Schmemann referred to as a culture that defines man "not from 'above' but from 'below.'" If we are merely the meat puppets our world tells us we are, there is no cost for safety that is too high.

Of course no one wants to get sick, or to be responsible for the sickness of another. But there was a time (not even very long ago) when we understood in Whose hands our fates were held. You cannot hold your own fate in your hands, though we do try. It's a bit like giving yourself a piggyback ride.

One has the sense that there is a communal waiting for victory, for all of this to end and for things to return to "normal." That, too, is a fantasy. A veil has been pulled aside, and what has been revealed to us is what was true all along – that we are fragile; that we live in a fallen world in which bodies sicken and die; that *we* will sicken and die in time, long or short. But the battle has already been won. We can see that, as McGinley so ably points out, if we cast our eyes above, rather than below.

Matt Scanlon, Falls Church, Virginia

CLIMATE CONVERSION

On Cardinal Peter Turkson's "The Spiritual Roots of Climate Crisis": This interview with Cardinal Peter Turkson should be required reading for political leaders the world over. If we stop for a moment to think of God's wonderful creation – where the fruits of the earth were to be shared by all – and see what, in our selfishness, we have done, we need to hang our heads in shame. To put it bluntly, we have made a mess of God's wonderful creation and unfortunately the innocent are paying the highest price.

Mervyn Anthony Maciel,
Surrey, England

THE FOUNDATION OF HOPE

On David Bentley Hart's "Tradition and Disruption": David Bentley Hart's wonderfully crafted article is provocative, slippery, and, perhaps, a bit of flummery. His work begins with the notion that the church's effort to rightly articulate the gospel was something that occurred long after the existence and work of the earliest, kingdom-intoxicated, Christians. But the questions that finally led to the creeds began during the life of Jesus, when he asked his disciples: "Who do men say that I am?"

It appears that the earliest of Christians loved God with their minds as well as their hearts. This was so because the center of the proclamation of the gospel (Acts 2 and I Corinthians 15) was the coming and work of Jesus Christ. It is true, of course, that invested in this proclamation was (and is!) the coming of the kingdom of God. It is also true that this coming will mean the utter disruption of this present, wicked age and thus inspires a kind of rebellion on the part of God's people.

But there always has been a center to godly Christian rebellion, because there is a center to the gospel and that center is Jesus Christ. From this center, the kingdom of God was understood (and not in a hazy way!); by the reality of this center the kingdom of God was expected; from this center the claims of nations and rulers were tested and adjudicated.

Thus we understand that Christian refusal to embrace racism (or the policy of abortion on demand) comes not from a sense of an unknowable disruption caused by the future coming of the kingdom of God. Instead, it comes from an understanding of the nature and implication of the Incarnation. It

comes from knowing that the creed we profess on Sunday morning is true. Now we can see that the creed is not simply a "melancholy" response to the delay of the coming of the kingdom. It is, instead, an articulation of the gospel, and when it is understood, it leads Christians to act in a way that is congruent to the reality of this gospel; a reality that will mark the coming kingdom, a kingdom reality we can know, because we know the king.

To declare the creed is to declare light in the midst of darkness, truth in the midst of a great lie, the foundation of hope in the midst of despair. Furthermore, because the creed declares the truth, we are emboldened to await the coming kingdom with certainty.

Michael Frank, Pipestem, West Virginia

A CAREGIVER'S DILEMMA

On Johann Christoph Arnold's "Living with Dementia," plough.com*: I am grateful that you are helping people think about dementia. However, I felt that the article was excessively negative against care homes. My wife has frontotemporal dementia (FTD); she

was diagnosed over fourteen years ago. She is still at home, but the time is probably coming soon when the loving thing to do is place her. At present I am able to care for her needs (cooking, cleaning, dressing, coping with double incontinence) but if her limited mobility decreases any more I might not be physically able to care for her as she needs. At that point I believe the loving thing to do would be to place her in care where people are around all the time and can recharge by going home after their shift is over. The alternative would be to provide sub-standard care at home.

Such a placement would not be, in my opinion, giving up on her care, nor on my wedding vows, but a shifting into a new role whereby I would still advocate for her. After all, if our loved one has a medical emergency we don't insist on caring for them in our house, but are willing to let them go to hospital.

In my experience the life of a caregiver is hard and often very lonely, and there is the temptation to feel unnecessary guilt when faced with having to choose from a number of bad choices. I felt that the author was trying to pile on unnecessary guilt using inflammatory language such as "warehouse" and "feel guilt, pain, and shame." This very negative approach to caregivers spoiled what was otherwise a good article.

Stephen Guy Longley, Korpoströmsvägen, Finland

db Waterman, *Freestyler*, collage and acrylic on paper, 2021 (detail)

FAMILY& FRIENDS
AROUND THE WORLD

Photograph by Trudi Brinkmann

Home in My Heart
Trudi Brinkmann

Mountains surround the Bruderhof community in Yeongwol, South Korea.

Somewhere in my first few months of learning Korean, I was listening to my usual grammar lessons when the speaker introduced an expression that I now often find myself inserting into English sentences – at least mentally.

When I see or hear something for the first time and I have a positive reaction to it, I can say in English, "I like it," whether it's music, clothing, food, or a place. In Korean, saying "I like [something]" indicates that I'm familiar with it already, and yes, I like it. A first sight of a pretty dress, a first listen to a hit song, a first view of a beautiful place, all merit the uniquely Korean expression, "It enters my heart." For those who read Korean: 마음에 들어요. For those who can't: *ma-eum-e dul-eoyo*.

Learning the Korean language is more than a self-inflicted mental challenge for me: I am privileged to be in South Korea, experiencing the beginnings of a small Bruderhof community of about twenty people ranging from five to eighty-five years old: foreigners and Koreans, families and singles. Initially, we lived in separate apartment buildings in the city of Taebaek. Earlier this year, we all moved to a countryside property in Yeongwol to better share a communal life and welcome visitors. With help from neighbors, we're learning which vegetables grow best, how much rain monsoons bring, how much one local rooster can crow, and more.

By now, days fly by quickly in Yeongwol, but they didn't at first. One April morning, I woke up to the sound of rain pattering on the carport roof below my window. I love that sound. April showers aren't assumed in Korea; springtime is a dry season complete with wildfires. Additionally, dust blowing in from China's vast deserts (not to mention the airborne import of "made in China" pollution) makes rain a welcome air purifier and fire extinguisher.

Raindrops spoke comfort but didn't wash away the nagging feeling that this

Trudi Brinkmann lives at Yeongwol, a Bruderhof community in South Korea.

wasn't home. I'm a nature lover, so the imposing mountains, the river, the big sky, should have grabbed my heart, but their charms had only gotten detached mental acknowledgement from me. Evening jogs lacked their usual pleasure: I missed having large apartment buildings nearby, the sound of a train pausing traffic, the brightly lit little storefronts, the small, easy-to-climb mountains, and the people – those I knew and those I didn't. I knew my new home had to take root in my heart at some point. I just needed time and a catalyst.

I got up to take a pre-breakfast walk in the pattering rain. I took a now-familiar route down the road, across the bridge, and back. Something happened. The white mist gently suspended near the tops of the dark gray-green mountains and the silver-highlighted river caught my heart. *Ma-eum-e dul-eoyo. It enters my heart.* I didn't know the place well yet and I wouldn't have thought a gray morning could have such bewitching beauty. But it did. Something clicked and my new home felt like, well, *home.*

Once more, the season pauses a moment, as if giving me a chance to catch up. Almost as if aware that their deep green summer look is getting old, the mountainside trees grab my attention again with autumnal brilliance. Yellows and oranges, dark pines and bright red maples match my memories of autumns in New York. With the spreading colors, my own sense of belonging is growing. The river, teeming with large birds (that everyone else can name), captivates me as much as each subtle sunset beyond the dusty blue mountains. At night, the stars seem closer than before.

My old home still holds a firm and special place in my heart, but it has moved over to share the space. I like this new home. It has entered my heart.

Remembering Alice von Hildebrand, 1923–2022
Erna Albertz

"If anything that I say is *not* true, I will gladly take the credit for it; it is entirely my own error. If, however, I say something true, I can claim no responsibility. It has only come through me from above." I am sitting on a spongy sofa while Dr. Alice von Hildebrand ("Lily" to me and my companions) perches wren-like on a hard, straight-backed chair directly in front of us, our knees almost touching. It is 2011 and we're meeting in her home in New Rochelle, New York. Her hands are in constant motion, the gestures a perfect complement to her thick Belgian accent.

We are leaning toward one another, partly out of necessity since at eighty-eight Lily is hard of hearing, but also because I don't want to miss a word. From the moment the three of us stepped into her apartment, she had taken charge, 100 percent the philosophy professor, leading us straight to the sofa and pulling up her chair. We hadn't known what to expect of this first meeting, but immediately realized here was someone so passionate about the highest questions of life that it was not going to be a relaxing chat over a cup of tea.

Lily herself described this intensity perfectly when speaking of her late husband, Catholic philosopher Dietrich von Hildebrand: "It was marriage on stilts." She felt she needed intellectual stilts to be able to reach his level. Well, Lily must have had some pretty serviceable ones, because while she would often say with a self-deprecating chuckle that "in all things practical we made a pathetic pair," in philosophical and spiritual matters she and Dietrich were true partners, spurring on one another's output of books and articles. Pope Pius XII called him "Doctor of the Church of the Twentieth Century," while Pope Francis made her Dame Grand Cross of the Order of St. Gregory, a papal knighthood.

Now, as we strain to keep up on our own mental stilts, Lily's charm and wit pull us along. It is easy to see why, during her career at Hunter College, she'd been voted best professor by her students.

In 1940, when she was just seventeen, Lily fled her native Belgium for the United States. Along the way, a near miss with a Nazi submarine led to a sublime experience. "I had the clear sense that I had 'touched eternity,' where time vanishes and everything is present," she wrote in her 2014 *Memoirs of a Happy Failure*. With this renewed perspective she applied herself to philosophy and theology, studying with Dietrich at

Erna Albertz lives at the Gutshof, a Bruderhof community in Austria.

Alice von
Hildebrand,
July 2017

Fordham University and collaborating with him till his death in 1977. For the next forty-five years she continued their life's work until she passed away. Instead of biological children, she regarded the many young people she swept into her orbit as sons and daughters. I and several of my fellow Bruderhof members were among them. Despite the difference between our Anabaptism and her Catholicism, our common desire to serve Christ immediately bonded us. We were able to share her thoughts on womanhood, immortality, love, and suffering on *plough.com*.

She, in turn, took us into her heart, often saying, "Tell me something beautiful about the Bruderhof," and delighting in whatever anecdotes we offered. Lily never neglected to pass on her greetings to our elders or to pray for them, entering as fully as possible into our lives and inviting us into hers. One of us, Vivian Warren, accompanied her on several trips, and I stayed with her in her apartment to provide care and companionship after she broke a hip.

What is the first thing you would do upon arriving home from the hospital? Relax,

focus on gathering strength; perhaps eat a real meal. Not Lily. She headed straight for her computer to painstakingly type an article she had been putting together in her head. She was extremely concerned for America and its direction, for moral relativism and respect for life, and prayed for her adopted country many hours each day.

Lily also grappled with Jesus' last prayer that all believers would be one (John 17:21) and the seeming impossibility of it. Perhaps this was one reason she opened her doors to us.

I asked a few of Lily's Bruderhof "daughters" to share their remembrances. Alison recalls Lily's fundamental gratefulness and "symphony of thank-yous," as she put it, for every little thing. Carmen points to Lily's joy in sharing — "a meal, a piece of chocolate, the Gospel" — and a favorite prayer by Saint Teresa of Ávila she often recited:

> Let nothing disturb you,
> Let nothing frighten you,
> All things are passing away:
> God never changes.
> Patience obtains all things.
> Whoever has God lacks nothing;
> God alone suffices.

Thinking of the turmoil and confusion that this prayer answers, Louise writes of Lily's hope that God's truth would prevail: "I saw that her belief in God as the only truth was what held her through everything she encountered. Lily knew that God was the ultimate power and so she lived in simple, humble obedience. This is something any one of us can do."

I remember Lily telling me, "Just as in the gospel we have the story of the woman who said, 'The dogs eat the crumbs that the children let fall,' even a *crumb* of God's truth can enrich our souls, and it's only in eternity that we're going to see the whole body of it."

Lily once defined a saint as "someone who, through God's grace, *sees*." Now she can surely see, and like a good mother she has channeled her spiritual resources well to provide us with plenty of nourishing bread until we too can join her at its Source.

Poet in This Issue

Ned Balbo's six books include *The Cylburn Touch-Me-Nots* (New Criterion Poetry Prize) and *3 Nights of the Perseids* (Richard Wilbur Award). He has received grants or fellowships from the National Endowment for the Arts (translation) and the Maryland Arts Council. From 2015–18 he was a visiting faculty member in Iowa State University's MFA program in creative writing and environment. In July 2021 he was a Mid-Atlantic Arts Foundation Fellow at the Virginia Center for the Creative Arts. Recent poems appear in *American Journal of Poetry, Christian Century, The Common, Ecotone, Ginkgo Prize 2019 Ecopoetry Anthology*, and elsewhere. He is married to poet and essayist Jane Satterfield. See his poem "Blessing the Bells" on page 49, and "Autumn in Chrysalis-Time" on page 55.

Photograph by Erna Albertz

FORUM ≋
RESPONSES TO ERIKA BACHIOCHI

Photograph courtesy of Library of Congress

THE FUTURE OF PRO-LIFE

Just after the decision overturning *Roe* and *Casey* was leaked, *Plough* published a piece by legal scholar Erika Bachiochi entitled "After *Roe v. Wade* and *Dobbs v. Jackson*," in which she called readers to heed the wisdom of nineteenth-century women's rights activists in navigating a world where abortion is again illegal in many states. The following letters, from activists, scholars, and journalists, respond to her piece (*plough.com/AfterRoe*).

Leah Libresco Sargeant, *Other Feminisms substack:* I'm grateful for Erika Bachiochi's exploration of the work of turn-of-the-century feminists who supported women and opposed abortion. Some modern social justice movements, by contrast, tend toward the transhuman – they aim to liberate human beings from any limit on who we can be or what we can do. Any restriction is suspect.

In essence, many modern activists look for freedom *from being human*. Thus, a feminism shaped by these views doesn't advocate for the freedom of women to be women in the world. Instead, it advocates for the right of women to be free of the burdens of *being women*.

While early pro-life feminists saw a man's ability to walk away from a child he'd fathered as a grave moral fault, present-day feminism often sees the ability to walk away as the basic prerequisite to being an equal citizen.

Their argument depends on seeing the basic unit of society as the lone unencumbered citizen.

This view sells everyone, not just women, short. Our ties to each other are not an "extra" or a luxury good. But when we put the unattached person at the center of our anthropology, our connections to each other are dismissed as optional: "If you couldn't support a baby, a friendship, a marriage, you shouldn't have had one!" All of us begin our lives dependent, and we depend on each other even as adults for help in caring for the vulnerable people in our lives.

Ayala H., *Mizrahi-American writer (@prolifejewess):* "Men's sexual appetites . . . and subsequent lack of responsibility often put women in a position where they felt powerless to refuse, and were left to deal with the consequences on their own." That's one of the most important sentiments

for pro-life activists to remember in a post-*Roe* world. Bachiochi eloquently connects the source of anti-natalism with the horrors it leads to.

I was born in 2003. The feminism I grew up with looks very different from that which Bachiochi describes. The original movement was intentionally subverted by anti-natalists in the sixties and seventies to pursue the vision of the sexual revolution. Recently, feminists like Sue Ellen Browder have brought to light the lobbying that went into that change. Looking at today's women's movement, it's undeniable how pervasive that change has been.

When I walk into feminist spaces today, I'm greeted with the narrative that women's bodies exist to be used. If a woman isn't willing to have casual sex with strangers or perform alienating labor for a corporation, she has internalized misogyny.

Many male "feminists," to my horror, proudly echo the beliefs of the man who raped me when I was fifteen. To them, women are not powerful nurturers, but rather jeans to be unbuckled and muscles to be exhausted. There is no respect for the almost divine ability to create life, only scorn at the resources that a child takes from the female body and, subsequently, its sexual capacity. In the horrible eventuality that a woman does begin to nurture new life as a result of one of these sexual encounters? Men are free to dump us at the abortion clinic and move on to the next body. After all, they're pro-choice.

A young parader in a New York City suffragist parade, 1912

This cycle has to end. Going forward, we must recognize the connection between the abuse of women and anti-natalism. It is imperative that pro-life activists take back feminism, respect female sexuality, and hold men accountable for their treatment of women. A culture of life will not exist until women and our children are valued above corporate and sexual demands.

Alexandra DeSanctis Marr, *Ethics and Public Policy Center (Washington, DC):* Erika Bachiochi – my colleague at the Ethics and Public Policy Center – offers a thoughtful case for how pro-lifers can make abortion appear less attractive by supporting women in difficult circumstances. This is a noble and necessary goal. As important as it is to offer legal protection to unborn children, we must also acknowledge the importance of reducing or eliminating the perceived need for abortion.

This latter goal is arguably more difficult than enacting policies to protect unborn children. Bachiochi is right that desperation often contributes to a woman's choice to have an abortion, but it's imperative to remember that no desperation justifies abortion. Whether a woman suffers due to poverty, lack of support from the child's father, or the absence of a social safety net, violence against her child is never acceptable, nor is it a solution to any of these woes.

As Bachiochi notes, early feminists believed abortion was not only an abdication of responsibility toward one's child, and therefore morally wrong, but also that legal abortion would harm women themselves. That

prediction has certainly come true. The economists George Akerlof, Janet Yellen, and Michael L. Katz write in a 1996 article in the *Quarterly Journal of Economics* that the widespread acceptance of abortion and contraception has led to a decline in "shotgun" marriages, which in turn has led to increases in child poverty and a trend they call the "feminization of poverty." "By making the birth of the child the physical choice of the mother, the sexual revolution has made marriage and child support a social choice of the father," they write.

There is certainly room for pro-lifers to debate the best ways to support women in need so that abortion doesn't appear to be the best available solution. As Ryan Anderson and I argue in our new book *Tearing Us Apart*, a crucial piece of the puzzle is becoming educated about the many ways that abortion has harmed women and learning to communicate that reality to those who believe abortion is a boon.

Charles C. Camosy, *Creighton University School of Medicine:* Erika Bachiochi is the rare academic who is meticulous

in getting the history right, and also bold in drawing lessons for our present day.

And if there were ever a moment for her voice to be heeded, it's now. Our current realignment, offering an astonishing level of creative political ferment, provides the pro-life movement with a rare opportunity to listen to the feminists of the nineteenth century. Indeed, now is probably the best time for this message to break through since the early 1980s, when large swaths of the pro-life movement signed up for Reagan-style fusionism, making alliances that compromised their pro-life principles.

Pro-lifers have a duty to emulate these feminists' refusal to choose between seeking prenatal justice and addressing the underlying factors that most frequently drive vulnerable women to seek abortions. Indeed, the two goals reinforce each other.

I'd add one further point drawn from Catholic social teaching's insistence on a preferential option for the poor. That teaching means following Bachiochi and the first-wave feminists on robust social supports for the economically vulnerable. But it also means taking the views of the poor seriously. Significantly, it is the privileged classes who are most supportive of abortion rights: the more vulnerable classes tend to support prenatal justice at a higher rate. Listening to the "missing voices" in our abortion discourse means listening to people who are disproportionately anti-abortion.

Maria Oswalt, *Rehumanize International and* Life Matters Journal*:* "The poor cry out for justice and equality and we respond with legalized abortion. . . . I believe that in a society that permits the life of even one individual (born or unborn) to be dependent on whether that life is 'wanted' or not, all citizens stand in danger."

I've been reflecting on these words since the historic overruling of *Roe* and *Casey* at the end of June. They were written just one year before the *Roe v. Wade* decision, in 1972, by Graciela Olivárez, a Mexican-American feminist and lawyer who served on the Presidential Commission on Population Growth and the American Future.

As a Hispanic woman, I've always admired Olivárez's courage; she was one of just two members of the commission to dissent from the group's recommendation of abortion as a form of population control. She grasped a truth missed by many well-meaning people: rather than alleviating inequality, legal abortion perpetuates it.

The United States has a long, sordid history of controlling the reproductive decisions of women, particularly women of color, and the poor. From sexual violence against enslaved women, to the dangerous contraceptive experiments performed upon Puerto Rican women, to "Mississippi appendectomies" and other forms of forced sterilization, every generation in our nation's history has witnessed horrific reproductive injustice.

In light of this, I can understand why some might be fearful of how restricting abortion will impact these marginalized populations. However, abortion is not a decision like choosing whether to use contraception or to seek sterilization. Abortion ends the life of a human being. It is a form of

violence, called "legal murder" by civil rights icon Fannie Lou Hamer, who was forcibly sterilized in 1961. Hamer understood the pain of reproductive injustice; that knowledge informed her view that legal abortion was yet another attempt to control the black community by killing their children. In her words, "Nobody's free until everybody's free," and she really meant everybody – even the unborn.

In the fifty years since Olivárez wrote her dissent, marginalized communities have lost millions of lives to legal abortion, and income inequality in the United States has only worsened. Black and brown communities are still disproportionately impacted by poverty and violence, including the violence of abortion: nationwide, black infants are aborted at five times the rate of white ones, and black mothers face atrocious disparities in healthcare. While the overturning of *Roe* isn't going to immediately solve these problems – we still have a long way to go to end legal abortion in every state – I have hope it is a step in the right direction. When we expand protections for the vulnerable, we all win. Low-income families and women of color deserve true justice, and in a post-*Roe* world, we can make sure that includes holistic, nonviolent reproductive justice.

Erika Bachiochi *responds:* Since *Plough* published my article, the Supreme Court has released its official opinion in *Dobbs v. Jackson Women's Health*, overturning *Roe v. Wade* and *Planned Parenthood v. Casey*.

Unsurprisingly, Justices Breyer, Kagan, and Sotomayor wrote an autonomy-

oriented dissenting opinion, suggesting that without the constitutional right to abortion, women were relegated to second-class citizenship. This line is particularly noteworthy: "Most women in 1868 had a foreshortened view of their rights: if most men could not then imagine giving women control over their bodies, most women could not imagine having that kind of autonomy."

Had the dissenters bothered to research the views of the women's rights advocates of that time, they'd have found that these women spoke and wrote frequently about controlling their own bodies. They just didn't think that control extended to violating others' bodies: those of their own children.

Each of the wonderful commentators sees the possibility of, as Maria Oswalt puts it, a "holistic, nonviolent reproductive justice." This is solidarity, authentic justice; it is the dissenting justices who have a foreshortened view of our rights. For the early feminists, our rights were not grounded in male-normed ideals of unencumbered "autonomy," but in our common human responsibility to care for one another.

As obstetrician and gynecologist Alice Bunker Stockham wrote in 1887: "By what false reasoning does she convince herself that another life, still more dependent upon her for its existence, with equal rights and possibilities, has no claim upon her for protection?" It's the false reasoning of a society built, for more than a half century, on misogynist lies. It's now our time to rebuild – and on solid ground. ➢

Image public domain

CLARE STOBER

Retooling the Plough

We're giving our logo a bit of an edge. Here's why.

DID YOU NOTICE anything different on the front cover of this issue? If so, you've caught our new logo, created to hold its own in any corner, while giving the artwork its due. Don't worry, it is not heralding some shift in our core beliefs. If anything, this design move has taken us closer to our own roots.

Illumination from the Luttrell Psalter, fourteenth century

Plough started in Germany in 1920 as a biweekly magazine, *Das neue Werk* (The New Work), published by the intentional community now known as the Bruderhof. From the start, the editors had a penchant for agricultural imagery; early publications included *Der Pflug* (The Plough) and *Junge Saat* (Young Seed). Already in 1917, founding editor Eberhard Arnold had written, in his previous post as editor of *Die Furche* (The Furrow):

> Only where the plow of God has tilled our lives can sowing bear fruit. An enduring deepening of the interior life can be brought about only through the plowing of repentance. Therefore our main task is to work for that spiritual revolution and re-evaluation

which leads to *metanoia* – the fundamental transformation of mind and heart.

And that's what this small community worked to do, publishing books as well as the magazine, such as a volume on the early church and an in-depth series of *Quellen*, "source books" of Christian writings from earlier centuries. These were no closed-door efforts run by an editorial team; the whole community could be found reading the drafts aloud while sorting and preparing potatoes for the next day's meal, a lively discussion flying around with the peelings.

One can imagine Else von Hollander, one of three founding Bruderhof members and an artist with a gift for layout and lettering, working late on a book cover design. Perhaps it was she who first chose the bold typeface that announced some of our titles then, and has come full circle to introduce our magazine now. We know that in its earliest days, the publishing house established a relationship with Rudolf Koch, a leading German designer still famous today for creating a number of typefaces, one of which is

---

Clare Stober is creative director at Plough *and the editor of* Another Life Is Possible. *She is a member of the Bruderhof and lives at Fox Hill in Walden, New York.*

prosaically named Fette Deutsche Schrift (Fat German Font).

Eberhard, Else, and others spent long days on the road speaking at conferences, calling on contributors, and raising awareness for their publishing efforts and communal venture. The urgency grew under the shadow of the Third Reich, and their efforts did not go unnoticed.

In 1936, facing increasing harassment by the Gestapo, the community shipped its printing press to England. In 1938, only a year after the German publishing house and its supporting Bruderhof community were shuttered by an SS raid, the magazine appeared in English under the name *The Plough*.

Apart from being the name of every other British and Irish pub, the name *Plough* had additional resonance in the magazine's new home. In the British Isles, the constellation Ursa Major (known to North Americans as the Big Dipper) is the Plough, guiding the farmer starting early or working late. And in British literature, from the fourteenth-century *Piers Plowman* to John Masefield's 1911 poem "The Everlasting Mercy," Christ himself guides the blade: "O ploughman of the sinner's soul. / O Jesus, drive the coulter deep / To plough my living man from sleep."

The Plough's logo must have been sketched by a member of the new community in the Cotswolds, where dozens of English pacifists were joining the German refugees. In February 1940 Eric Gill, creator of the Gill Sans typeface and an early advocate of distributism along with G. K. Chesterton, submitted drafts of a new Plough logo. His design was never implemented; shortly afterward, the community was forced to leave England amid wartime panic.

Plough Publishing House has been based in the United States since 1963. In 2013, it moved

Plough

to new offices at Fox Hill Bruderhof in Walden, New York. A year later it relaunched its flagship quarterly print magazine, featuring the same motif that had appeared on the first 1938 cover.

Two years ago, *Plough*'s editors and designers agreed that it was time to refresh the design, especially the logo and typography. Now change has come to the cover and website. Our designers have always wished that the word "Plough" and logo didn't take up a third of the cover; a more compact nameplate would greatly expand the possibilities of art they could use. And as logos go, it's somewhat spindly – if you have to shrink it down, it doesn't "hold its space well."

After much consideration, we agreed that while the name – and its British spelling – weren't up for a change, the old hand-guided plow was. Design challenges aside, it's less recognizable to readers than it was in 1938. (Those of us who aren't farmers might not even know that plowing has fallen out of favor!)

THOUGH WE ARE PARKING the plow, we're not abandoning our heritage. Poring through our archives and original book covers, I saw the prevalence of Rudolf Koch's bold Fette Deutsche Schrift and found that my predecessors in the 1920s had purchased this very font – as handset type made of lead. I adapted the uppercase P to create *Plough*'s new-old logo. To accompany the calligraphic P, I designed a stronger "Plough" wordmark in a contemporary condensed serif font. We've combined the two in the new nameplate you can see on the cover of this issue. We hope that it will call out to readers from an array of magazines on a table, or a line of book spines on a shelf, with the bold challenge you have come to expect from *Plough*, and others have yet to discover. ➤

Ivan Vdovin / Alamy Stock Photo

PETER MOMMSEN

Word Is Bond

In a culture addicted to endless choice, vows offer a higher freedom.

Marc Chagall, *Abraham and Three Angels*, 1966

THE FOUNDING CHARTER of modern liberal democracy, the American Declaration of Independence, famously names "Life, Liberty and the pursuit of Happiness" as rights that all people possess by divine ordinance. These rights, it says, are "unalienable" – none can abolish or waive them. This trio of rights shapes not only American civic life but the political systems of countries that the Declaration's signatories 246 years ago could never have imagined embracing them.

Yet in recent years, doubts have been growing across the political spectrum about how well the last two on the list fit together, if they fit at all. It's not obvious that unfettered liberty is even compatible with happiness,

especially if one understands happiness in the robust classical sense familiar to the American Founders: happiness as complete human flourishing, the *eudaimonia* of Aristotle. Modern people are freer – legally, socially, romantically, and as consumers – than ever before in human history. But increasing numbers of people on both the left and right question whether unprecedented freedom might be leading to less flourishing, not more. They are dissatisfied with an atomized way of life that offers endless choices of goods, services, and experiences (at least to those with enough money) but undermines the ties of solidarity and mutuality that humankind requires for happiness. They yearn for more heroic virtues, more sacrificial commitments, more comprehensive visions of the individual and common good.

Political philosophers sometimes call this set of concerns "post-liberalism," a label that sounds abstract. Yet these yearnings aren't just theoretical. For example, they are bundled together with the movements for national conservatism that have gained influence in countries from India to Brazil to Poland. Many exponents, including the Hungarian president Viktor Orbán, explicitly reject the liberty-focused ideals of the American founding. Here in the United States, such ideas often go hand in hand with what is called "Christian nationalism" – originally a term of opprobrium, but one that some adherents now embrace.

Movements on the left respond to similar impulses, though in a far different register. Take for example the passionate moralities of social justice – "wokeism" to their critics – that have reshaped many Western norms and institutions over the past decade. While in colloquial speech these moralities are "liberal" as opposed to conservative, they mark a turn from the live-and-let-live permissiveness of classical liberalism to a more demanding ethic – one manifested by speech rules on university campuses, implicit bias trainings at work, and Diversity, Equity, and Inclusion mandates from government.

Both expressions of post-liberalism are born of a sense that too much liberty is harmful to social well-being, while differing in their focus on which members of society are most at risk. But the sense has also emerged that excess freedom is harmful to *oneself*. This helps account for why Jordan B. Peterson, the Canadian Jungian psychologist, has found millions of readers and YouTube viewers by recommending self-discipline as an "antidote to chaos." This chaos, he clarifies in his bestselling 2018 book *Twelve Rules for Life*, is the direct result of modernity's "untrammeled freedom." (Politically, Peterson remains a classical liberal.)

Left-wing activists, conservative nationalists, and Jungian self-helpers obviously disagree about many things. Yet they share at least one intuition in common: humans need binding commitments and hard boundaries, for others' good and for their own. Private and public happiness, if it's to mean more than mere license for pleasure-seeking, requires giving up the untrammeled freedom to do whatever one wants.

DESPITE THESE COUNTERCURRENTS, the unfixed conditions of modernity are still the water that most of us swim in. In his 2000 book *Liquid Modernity*, Zygmunt Bauman observed:

> Forms of modern life may differ in quite a few respects – but what unites them all is precisely their fragility, temporariness, vulnerability and inclination to constant change. To "be modern" means to modernize – compulsively, obsessively; not so much just "to be," let alone to keep its identity intact, but forever "becoming," avoiding completion, staying underdefined. Each new structure which replaces the previous one as soon as it is declared old-fashioned and past its use-by date is only another momentary settlement – acknowledged as temporary and "until further notice."

In Bauman's account, "liquid modernity" is more a matter of large-scale social patterns than individual behavior. But these patterns have created a script for life in which change is the only constant. The unexamined article of faith is the categorical imperative to keep your options open. This imperative underlies the habits of consumerism and instant gratification that fuel modern capitalism. And it feeds a general reluctance to make commitments, a refusal to be pinned down for the long term.

Consider the decline of three forms of commitment that involve giving up options, each with deep roots in Western culture: marriage, military service, and monastic life. Marriage rates, to start with, have been dropping around the world for decades; in the United States, they have halved over the past fifty years. In tandem, cohabitation outside marriage has increased dramatically, but not enough to make up for the dearth of weddings, and with a corresponding increased risk that a subsequent marriage will break up: US couples who cohabit before marrying are more likely to divorce. In many countries, divorce rates skyrocketed in the 1970s and peaked in the 1980s, and despite declining somewhat in places since then, globally they remain historically high, with the United Nations reporting a general upward trend. As marriage gets rarer, for a couple to make lifelong vows of faithfulness is no longer a given. In Western countries, a vocal minority champions open marriage and polyamory, with some criticizing even voluntary monogamy as oppressive in itself.

Military enlistment, too, is in trouble; fewer than one in ten young Americans say they would consider joining up. Just since the start of the pandemic, the share of young adults the US military classes as potentially willing to enlist has fallen by nearly a third, from 13 to 9 percent. Those committed to Christian nonviolence (as this magazine is) might be expected to celebrate the drop – and to the extent that it reflects a rejection of killing, we do. Yet opposition to war doesn't seem to be the main reason why the US Army, for example, has only managed to recruit a fraction of the new soldiers it needs this year. Nor does the fact that only a quarter of young Americans are both physically fit enough and lack a disqualifying criminal record. The root cause seems to be that fewer are open to even entertaining the idea of committing to serve.

Monastic professions have been declining for far longer. Catholic monks and nuns account for the vast majority of people in religious life, and since the 1960s their numbers have fallen precipitously around the world, most dramatically in North America and Europe. To be sure, in a few Latin American and African countries, monasticism continues to thrive, and even in the United States, a handful of orders, most of them traditionalist, still attract postulants. But they are outliers. Since 1965, the number of men in US Catholic orders has fallen by over half, while the number of Catholic sisters has dropped by more than three-quarters. As with military service and marriage, the causes of these trends are complex, and often seem linked with specific crises within Catholicism. Even so, the global dimensions of the decline are striking.

THESE THREE EXAMPLES represent symptoms of a culture bent on avoiding commitment. Yet they also point to a way out of liquid modernity, as life scripts that remain available to any who wish to adopt them. At an even more basic level, they hint at a way in which liberty and happiness might be reconciled.

Significantly, each of these paths begins with the same step: freewillingly making a vow. Thus a monk or nun, after passing through postulancy, novitiate, and temporary profession, takes lifelong vows of chastity, poverty, and obedience to his or her community. Military recruits take an oath of enlistment, promising allegiance to their nation, a vow that isn't necessarily lifelong but comes with the understanding that they may die in the course of fulfilling it. At a wedding, in the archetypal vow, couples pledge faithfulness in health and in sickness, "till death do us part" (or they did until the vogue for writing DIY vows, which have been known to leave the crucial part out).

A vow is a declaration not of independence but of a bond. When we vow, we are giving up our future freedom. But this loss comes with a gain. As G. K. Chesterton writes:

Modern sages offer to the lover, with an ill-favored grin, the largest liberties and the fullest irresponsibility; but they do not respect him as the old Church respected him; they do not write his oath upon the heavens, as the record of his highest moment. They give him every liberty except the liberty to sell his liberty, which is the only one that he wants.

The higher excellence of the freedom of the vow is difficult for us moderns to accept on the basis of arguments, as Chesterton knew. But we can tell stories that illustrate it. First among these is the great narrative told by the writers of the Bible from Genesis to Revelation about the preeminent vow – the covenant between God and Israel, and by extension, between God and humankind. God calls Abraham, a man of no special importance, to leave behind everything he knows in his native Mesopotamian city, and gives him a promise in return:

> Go from your country and your kindred and your father's house to the land that I will show you. And I will make of you a great nation, and I will bless you and make your name great, so that you will be a blessing. I will bless those who bless you, and him who dishonors you I will curse, and in you all the families of the earth shall be blessed. (Gen. 12:1–3)

Abraham obeys, and the promise continues through Isaac, Jacob, and their descendants, to the present day. In the Christian understanding, God's promise finds fulfillment in Christ, the descendant of Abraham. Through him, all humankind is blessed – we are offered adoption into Abraham's family and the promise God made to him. The final book of the Christian Bible, drawing on the Hebrew prophets, even pictures this covenant as a marriage vow, fulfilled in the Marriage Supper of the Lamb.

For individual believers, the story of God's covenant with Abraham can be recapitulated in the stories of our own lives. To tell one such story, unremarkable except for the fact that I can tell it firsthand: As a twenty-one-year-old in my last year at college, I was a well-catechized believer in the liquid-modern creed. Though I

had grown up in the Bruderhof, the Anabaptist community that publishes this magazine, to me commitment-phobia came as easily as to any of my Gen X peers. I'd eagerly absorbed the meritocratic drive to chase socially desirable credentials and tokens of success. With that as my attitude, the communal life in which I'd grown up often felt confining. Studying at an Ivy League school seemed my ticket out into a world of boundless possibilities.

Yet on one particular day that sticks in my memory, the conviction forced itself on me that I was called to go back home and commit myself to this particular way of Christian discipleship. Membership in the Bruderhof is a lifetime commitment. It wasn't a flash of illumination, but rather a moment in a gradual process, like the slow clearing of water in a pool made muddy by disturbance. I went back to the Bruderhof after several years away and requested membership. Through the period of testing that followed, that conviction held. As Mother Teresa once said of women who had discerned a vocation: "They know. They know."

When the time for actually taking my vows finally came, it felt anticlimactic after all that had preceded it. The pastor presiding at the service was a genial Englishman in his eighties who had a marked tremor. ("The more John shakes, the more spiritual authority he gives off," is how my uncle used to describe it.) He asked me a series of questions based on centuries-old Anabaptist vows; at one point I remember him beaming as he paused for dramatic effect at each comma: "Do you surrender yourself completely, and do you bind yourself unreservedly, to God and to your brothers and sisters?" I said yes at the right places, and he shook my hand and sat down. That was it. I made my way back to my seat, and started the rest of my life.

Yet despite the lack of exalted emotions, that moment gave me a certainty that's stayed with me ever since: at least one decision has been made forever; one core question of life will no

longer keep coming up for revision or review. I'd given my word. After spending years frantically fending off any commitment that might limit my options, I was now bound.

And I soon discovered that being bound didn't feel like a loss of liberty. On the contrary, once the step had been taken, paralyzing daydreams about other possible life paths disappeared – not because of any sudden growth in spiritual maturity, but simply because the vow had itself changed who the vower was. It's a feeling that will be familiar to many newly married couples. To forsake all others, to make one's single irrevocable choice, creates a new freedom far better than the sterile freedom of endless options. It's a liberation that promises real happiness, a passage from just potentially living to becoming fully ourselves.

OF COURSE, VOWS DON'T ALWAYS work out that way. Even scripture tells stories of vows gone badly wrong. The grim tale of Jephtha in the Book of Judges stands out. As a military commander, Jephtha returns home from battle and has to sacrifice his daughter, his only child, to satisfy a rash vow he had made to help bring victory.

The problem of bad vows was long familiar to the Jewish sages: vows broken, vows unfulfilled, vows badly made. Given the important role that vow-making plays in the Hebrew scripture this isn't surprising. At some point in the early rabbinic era, the problem of bad vows became so acute that it called into being a remarkable rite. The Kol Nidre prayer is the centerpiece of the evening liturgy before Yom Kippur. Sung by a cantor as the congregation whispers along in an undertone, this penitential act frees worshipers from guilt for unfulfilled vows in preparation for the holiest day of the year.

One key to the Kol Nidre's power is aesthetic. According to Jonathan Sacks, the late chief rabbi of the United Kingdom, its "haunting music has the power like no other to unlock the gates of the Jewish heart." The unmistakable sighing melody, according to one legend, was handed down by God to Moses on Mount Sinai. More likely, the tune originated in the medieval Rhineland as a borrowing from the courtly minnesingers; it has since been made famous by composers from Beethoven to Bruch to Schoenberg.

Oddly, this prayer isn't really a prayer, and in fact never mentions God at all. Instead, notes Sacks, it is a "formula for undoing vows," lawyerly rather than devotional: "Never was there a deeper disconnect, a deeper dissonance, between the music and the words." In the form used in most Ashkenazi synagogues, its text dates to the 1100s, though with roots centuries earlier. In the service, the Aramaic words are repeated three times over:

> All vows, prohibitions, oaths, vows of dedication . . . that we have vowed, sworn, declared, and imposed upon ourselves from this Day of Atonement until the next Day of Atonement, may it come upon us for good. Regarding them all, we regret them. Let them all be released, forgiven, erased, null and void. They are not valid nor are they in force. Our vows are not our vows. Our prohibitions are not our prohibitions. Our oaths are not our oaths.

This rite was controversial from the first among leading rabbis. It seems to contradict the Torah's stern insistence that a vow, once spoken, must be fulfilled without fail. Scripture's exceptions – allowing a male householder to revoke vows made by a wife or daughter, and permitting the "redemption" of some vows through a monetary payment – prove the rule. Unsurprisingly then, the Kol Nidre was rejected by five out of the six Geonim, the highest authorities on Jewish law who shaped Talmudic interpretation in the seventh to eleventh centuries. Rabbinic qualms about the rite's validity have persisted ever since.

In later centuries in Europe, the Kol Nidre proved not just theologically dicey but downright dangerous. Its wording was quoted as grounds for doubting the veracity of Jews when they swore oaths in court or made promises in business, and became a pretext for legal discrimination and anti-Semitic violence. As a defensive response, some Jewish communities struck it from their prayer books until well into the twentieth century.

Yet the Kol Nidre has outlived its various detractors. One reason may be that despite appearing to negate the sacredness of vows, in fact it testifies to a deeper kind of fidelity. Rabbi Sacks has pointed out that the centuries when the Kol Nidre's popularity spread through Jewish communities were also the time of forced conversions of Jews under Christian (and sometimes Muslim) rulers. Here, in his view, the Kol Nidre played a needed role. Once a year, it gave conscience-stricken *conversos* the opportunity to enter the synagogue and, in the sight of God and their community, to undo their coerced oaths of apostasy. On the Day of Atonement, the unfaithful could at least declare their desire for faithfulness. For them, the Kol Nidre declared a trust that God stays true to his covenant even when humans prove false.

T HAT IS A PENITENTIAL STANCE which, in the Christian understanding, should be the attitude of every baptized believer. In our fallen state, every vow we make is irreducibly rash, no matter how carefully considered; we never know how the story of any vow will end. This applies with special force to the baptismal vow. Through baptism, every Christian has promised unconditional faithfulness to Christ; through sin, each stands as an apostate, reliant only on Christ's faithfulness.

Yet his faithfulness is enough, the New Testament assures us. In the words of the Letter to the Hebrews:

> Therefore, brethren, since we have confidence to enter the sanctuary by the blood of Jesus . . . let us hold fast the confession of our hope without wavering, for he who promised is faithful.

The grounds on which we dare to make our vows are no longer our own willpower or capacity for staying true, but God's. And so we are right to confidently make our pledge.

To this degree, then, it turns out that the American Founders were right: the Creator did endow us with an unalienable right of liberty. But he has endowed us with something else as well, a gift that is equally unalienable: desire for unreserved commitment of all we have and are. Our liberty is given us so that we in turn can freely dedicate ourselves to something greater. That's in fact what the signers of the Declaration of Independence did themselves, concluding their document with a vow that invokes "Divine Providence" as witness to "pledge to each other our Lives, our Fortunes and our sacred Honor."

Of course the upshot is not as simple as saying that any vow-making is better than none. That's plainly false, as Jephtha's example shows. Today it's easy to find causes and movements that prey on people's innate desire to give themselves to a higher allegiance in ways that are noxious and sinister.

But caution counsels discernment, not permanent indecision. Ultimately, to take a leap of commitment, even without knowing where one will land, is the only way to get to a happiness worth everything. It's the happiness described in the psalm that has long been recited in monastic communities when someone makes a lifelong vow: "This is my resting place for ever; here I will dwell, for I have desired it." ⤳

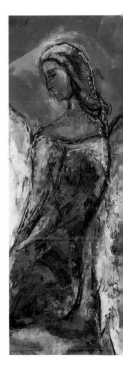

G. K. CHESTERTON

A Defense of Vows

Making vows is not for cowards.

Caspar David Friedrich, *The Watzmann*, 1825

THE MAN WHO MAKES a vow makes an appointment with himself at some distant time or place. The danger of it is that himself should not keep the appointment. And in modern times this terror of one's self, of the weakness and mutability of one's self, has perilously increased, and is the real basis of the objection to vows of any kind. . . .

Let us turn, on the other hand, to the maker of vows. The man who made a vow, however wild, gave a healthy and natural expression to the greatness of a great moment. He vowed, for example, to chain two mountains together, perhaps a symbol of some great relief of love, or aspiration. Short as the moment of his resolve might be, it was, like all great moments, a moment of immortality, and the desire to say

of it *exegi monumentum aere perennius* was the only sentiment that would satisfy his mind. The modern aesthetic man would, of course, easily see the emotional opportunity; he would vow to chain two mountains together. But, then, he would quite as cheerfully vow to chain the earth to the moon. And the withering consciousness that he did not mean what he said, that he was, in truth, saying nothing of any great import, would take from him exactly that sense of daring actuality which is the excitement of a vow. . . .

The revolt against vows has been carried in our day even to the extent of a revolt against the typical vow of marriage. It is most amusing to listen to the opponents of marriage on this subject. They appear to imagine that the ideal

Gilbert Keith Chesterton (1874–1936) was an English author of literary criticism, fiction, and theology.

of constancy was a yoke mysteriously imposed on mankind by the devil, instead of being, as it is, a yoke consistently imposed by all lovers on themselves. They have invented a phrase, a phrase that is a black and white contradiction in two words – "free-love" – as if a lover ever had been, or ever could be, free. It is the nature of love to bind itself, and the institution of marriage merely paid the average man the compliment of taking him at his word. Modern sages offer to the lover, with an ill-favored grin, the largest liberties and the fullest irresponsibility; but they do not respect him as the old Church respected him; they do not write his oath upon the heavens, as the record of his highest moment. They give him every liberty except the liberty to sell his liberty, which is the only one that he wants. . . .

It is exactly this backdoor, this sense of having a retreat behind us, that is, to our minds, the sterilizing spirit in modern pleasure. Everywhere there is the persistent and insane attempt to obtain pleasure without paying for it. Thus, in politics the modern Jingoes practically say, "Let us have the pleasure of conquerors without the pains of soldiers: let us sit on sofas and be a hardy race." Thus, in religion and morals, the decadent mystics say: "Let us have the fragrance of sacred purity without the sorrows of self-restraint; let us sing hymns alternately to the Virgin and Priapus." Thus in love the free-lovers say: "Let us have the splendor of offering ourselves without the peril of committing ourselves; let us see whether one cannot commit suicide an unlimited number of times."

Emphatically it will not work. There are thrilling moments, doubtless, for the spectator, the amateur, and the aesthete; but there is one thrill that is known only to the soldier who fights for his own flag, to the aesthetic who starves himself for his own illumination, to the lover who makes finally his own choice. And it is this transfiguring self-discipline that makes the vow a truly sane thing. It must have satisfied even the giant hunger of the soul of a lover or a poet to know that in consequence of some one instant of decision that strange chain would hang for centuries in the Alps among the silences of stars and snows. All around us is the city of small sins, abounding in backways and retreats, but surely, sooner or later, the towering flame will rise from the harbor announcing that the reign of the cowards is over and a man is burning his ships. ➤

Source: G. K. Chesterton, *The Defendant* (Dodd, 1904).

ABOUT US ≈

Plough is published by the Bruderhof, an international community of families and singles seeking to follow Jesus together. Members of the Bruderhof are committed to a way of radical discipleship in the spirit of the Sermon on the Mount. Inspired by the first church in Jerusalem (Acts 2 and 4), they renounce private property and share everything in common in a life of nonviolence, justice, and service to neighbors near and far. There are twenty-nine Bruderhof settlements in both rural and urban locations in the United States, England, Germany, Australia, Paraguay, South Korea, and Austria, with around 3000 people in all. To learn more or arrange a visit, see the community's website at *bruderhof.com*.

Plough features original stories, ideas, and culture to inspire faith and action. Starting from the conviction that the teachings and example of Jesus can transform and renew our world, we aim to apply them to all aspects of life, seeking common ground with all people of goodwill regardless of creed. The goal of *Plough* is to build a living network of readers, contributors, and practitioners so that, as we read in Hebrews, we may "spur one another on toward love and good deeds."

Plough includes contributions that we believe are worthy of our readers' consideration, whether or not we fully agree with them. Views expressed by contributors are their own and do not necessarily reflect the editorial position of *Plough* or of the Bruderhof communities. ➤

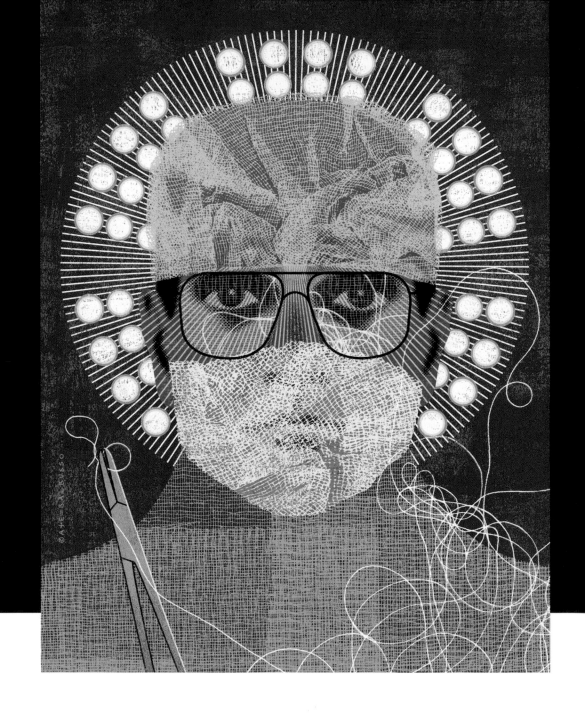

Bring Back Hippocrates

The Hippocratic Oath has largely disappeared from modern medicine. What have we lost?

LYDIA S. DUGDALE

"**D**O YOU THINK MEDICINE is actually a moral profession?"

I hadn't expected this question. She was a senior medical student of mine, and I knew that morality was important to her. She had grown up in a religious family and still practiced her faith. I was sure she understood her interactions with patients to be far more than mere transactions. How could she imagine for a moment that medicine *wasn't* a moral practice?

But she had good reason to ask. Medical school curricula change with the times, and no undergirding ethic prevails to explain medicine's telos. Apart from a few brief lectures on physician beneficence, patient autonomy, the doctrine of informed consent, and conflict of interest, medical education has very little to say on the topic of morality. The practice of medicine *appears* to be not much more than the exchange, for a fee, of "de-moralized" professional services – invigorated by the occasional

Artwork by
Anna and Elena
Balbusso, 2016

Lydia S. Dugdale is a physician and ethicist at Columbia University in New York City, and author of The Lost Art of Dying *(HarperOne, 2020).*

technological breakthrough and accompanied by a few tips on good customer service.

Of course, moving from the classroom to the hospital bed changes perspective. Patients

Medical school curricula change with the times, and no undergirding ethic prevails to explain medicine's telos.

presume their doctors seek their good and intend no harm. In fact, nothing carries more symbolic weight of this expectation than the Hippocratic Oath.

A case in point: while I was writing the previous paragraph, a young member of my family wandered into the office and inquired what I was writing. I told her and then asked, "Do you know what the Hippocratic Oath is?" She was quick to reply, "Of course. It's the oath that doctors take to become a doctor." Detecting some triumph in my expression, she began to doubt herself. "Well, isn't it?" she asked. "No," I replied. "It's the oath people *think* doctors take to become a doctor. In fact, most doctors don't."

In recent years, the Hippocratic Oath has been invoked to justify mandatory health-care

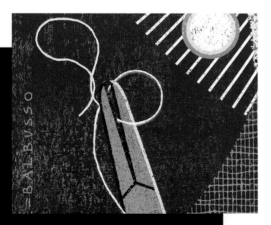

worker vaccination against Covid-19, and to insist on caring well for patients who treat doctors poorly. Conversely, when procedures go awry, it is not uncommon to hear frustrated patients reference the Hippocratic Oath and its famous injunction "first, do no harm." The truth is that the Hippocratic Oath does not say that the doctor should "first, do no harm." (That phrase appears in a different Hippocratic text, *Epidemics I*.) The myth of Hippocrates is more prolific than his oath.

THE HIPPOCRATIC OATH belongs to a collection of about seventy texts that compose the Hippocratic corpus. Some (but not all) are thought to have been penned by the ancient Greek paragon of doctoring, Hippocrates of Cos (ca. 460–370 BC). The writings are unified primarily by their Ionic Greek language, and they cover a range of topics, from questions of a physician's decorum and ethics to medical duties, descriptions of diseases, and accounts of patient experiences.

Hippocrates was contemporary to Socrates (ca. 470–399 BC). In the *Protagoras* the philosopher extols the good doctor – along with Phidias the sculptor and Homer the poet – as being what the scholar T. A. Cavanaugh calls "illustrative of the best of their kind."[1] If Phidias was a sculptor like no other, and Homer an unparalleled poet, the world had never seen the like of a physician such as Hippocrates. Even Aristotle, whose own father Nicomachus was physician to royalty, acknowledges in his *Politics* that Hippocrates is healer par excellence.

The renowned doctor hailed from the revered clan of the Asklepiads, devotees of Asklepios, demigod of health. Their circle was

1. T. A. Cavanaugh. *Hippocrates' Oath and Asclepius' Snake: The Birth of the Medical Profession* (New York: Oxford University Press, 2018): 33.

exclusive; only sons of physician members were admitted to learn medicine. They were famous for shunning quackery and for admitting what they could not cure. They could be trusted to attempt to treat only what they thought could be healed. And healing, for the Asklepiads, was understood to preclude killing. Hippocrates broke with the Asklepiad tradition by taking on promising students (in addition to sons) for a fee. His oath, then, begins with a covenant of sorts between physician and apprentice – important to establish if the mentee is not a blood relative – followed by a list of licit and illicit acts.

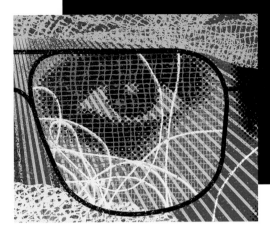

The young doctors swore before Apollo and a host of health-related gods and goddesses to "hold my teacher in this art equal to my own parents," to commit to prescribing only those diets that offered benefit to patients, to keep "pure and holy" in both life and art, and to help the sick. They also pledged to refrain from a host of activities, including:

– "all intentional wrong-doing and harm" to patients;
– breaching patient confidentiality;
– performing surgery for which they were not trained;
– causing abortion;
– poisoning or euthanizing patients or recommending such; and
– "abusing the bodies of man or woman, bond or free" (understood as sexual relations with patients).

The Greek word for "oath" – *horkos* – is related to the Greek word for "fence," *herkos*. The terms of an oath define the limits of – or "fence in" – the area for a particular activity. "Just as the bounds of a soccer pitch (or any field of play) allow the game to take place, an oath establishes boundaries for important activities," Cavanaugh notes in his book on the Hippocratic Oath.[2] In

2. Cavanaugh, *Hippocrates' Oath*, 43.

taking the oath of Hippocrates, the Asklepiads professed what was in and out of bounds. Fundamental to these bounds was the commitment to helping and not harming or killing patients or their fetuses.

NOT EVERY PHYSICIAN in antiquity swore the oath of Hippocrates. Legal and literary texts from the period suggest that some doctors had reputations as "unpunished killers," and the Hippocratic corpus itself contains texts that refer to abortifacients and

In a world with so little moral consensus, what guidelines can best serve a culture that can agree neither on the ends of medicine nor on what is permissible?

abortion technique. Even among Hippocrates' own followers, some denied that medicine's orientation toward healing precluded the taking of life. Nonetheless, in one of the rare references to the oath in classical medical literature, the physician Scribonius Largus (ca. AD 14–54) notes that Hippocrates forbade doctors from engaging in death-inducing activities. "How much more evil would he, who thought it wrong to destroy even the tenuous possibility of a man, judge the harming of a living human being?" After all, he adds, "medicine is the science of healing, not of harming."[3]

Although adherence to it was by no means universal, Hippocrates' oath continued to assert its influence throughout the Middle

The question is not simply whether the medical profession is moral, but what kind of morality it professes.

Ages. Some Christians thought the business of swearing to Greek gods meant the oath wasn't sufficiently Christian, so by the tenth century, a new version circulated replacing Greek divinities with the Christian God and strengthening its constraint on abortion. While it is difficult to know how many physicians ever took the oath, as of 1928 in the United States at least, only fourteen of seventy-nine medical schools required their students to swear the Hippocratic Oath in its original form.

IN CONTRAST WITH its historic significance and use, today no American medical student is required to take the Hippocratic Oath. Almost all medical schools administer some sort of oath, yet they share no consensus on a single text, and many select and revise their oath each year. Medical ethicists Audiey Kao and Kayhan Parsi, in the journal *Academic Medicine*, suggest that "the emergence of 'boutique' oaths can lead to fragmentation and confusion about the ethical values of the medical profession and, thus, dilute the value

3. Albert R. Jonsen, *A Short History of Medical Ethics* (New York: Oxford Univ. Press, 2000): 4–5.

of a professionally binding oath." If 104 medical schools take 107 different oaths (some swear two!) what core ethical precepts remain? When medical students complete training and still have no clear sense of what medicine is really *for*, then the profession of medicine has failed to *profess* – literally, "to declare openly" – what it is for. Or, at least, its professing is neither consistent nor loud enough for trainees to hear.

I routinely ask my students, "What's the goal, the telos, of medicine? What is medicine *for*?" I am most often met with a blank stare. Medical training tends to elide this question entirely. Is medicine for healing? For the restoration of wholeness? Does it include physical and mental health, or only physical? What about interventions that patients may desire that are not fundamentally oriented toward their health – the Brazilian butt lift, for example? To be sure, these questions are hotly contested where they are considered at all, and if teaching physicians fail even to bring them to the table, many young doctors never have the occasion to think through why they do what they do. Without having a sense of medicine's orientation it is difficult to discern its fences, to know what is in and out of bounds. But in a world with so little moral consensus, what guidelines can best serve a culture that can agree neither on the ends of medicine nor on what is permissible? If the Hippocratic Oath could not gain consensus in the fifth century BC, what are we to expect from our polarized world today?

The Hippocratic Oath lays a foundation for medicine's telos. Since the oath's clear goal is toward benefiting the sick, it makes sense for medicine as a profession to aim at restoring health. Such a teleological orientation, of course, is open to broad interpretation, but it offers a helpful starting point.

The oath also outlines doctors' fundamental duties toward patients – to help and

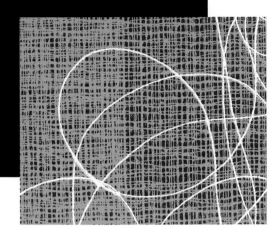

the course of trying to achieve those standards of excellence which are appropriate to, and partially definitive of, that form of activity, with the result that human powers to achieve excellence, and human conceptions of the ends and goods involved, are systematically extended."[4] If society wants the practice of medicine and the people it serves to flourish, then we must consider which activities will extend what is excellent, good, and purposeful about the practice, and choose not to pursue activities that corrode medicine.

not to harm. (Curiously, only 85 percent of commencement oaths pledge this.) You might ask, "What about the other elements of the oath? No abortion or euthanasia or sex with patients or divulging secrets?" While I certainly hope for consensus on the last two, most people today know that there is no consensus on the first two. However, even if society is unable to prohibit killing altogether, senior physicians might at least be able to train young doctors to consider every patient-oriented decision against the backdrop of restoring health and mitigating disease in a manner that helps and does not harm patients. This framing immediately eliminates the possibility of sexual relations with patients and breaching of confidentiality. Indeed, it demands even more: it requires moral reasoning by physician and patient together to adjudicate what is ultimately best for a patient's health – it underscores that medicine is fundamentally a *moral* practice.

Beyond identifying the aims of medicine and the duties of doctors, medical practitioners must consider what sort of *practice* medicine itself ought to be. The philosopher Alasdair MacIntyre defines a practice as "any coherent and complex form of socially established cooperative human activity through which goods internal to that form of activity are realized in

WHAT, THEN, OF OATH-TAKING? Is it necessary?

Here Cavanaugh offers several compelling reasons to take a medical oath.[5] The profession, he notes, deals in grave matters – vulnerability, sickness, and death – fitting for a solemn oath. (By contrast, it would be a stretch for cosmeticians to take solemn vows, he says.) Furthermore, a public oath demonstrates reflection, commitment, and deliberateness – its public nature encourages oath-takers to keep their promises. And finally, oaths define the field of play and focus subsequent deliberation. Oaths make clear what kind of art doctors practice.

My student was wise to ponder the moral nature of our work. And yet, the question is not simply whether the medical profession is moral, but what kind of morality it professes. In a divided world, physicians must seek unity on the fundamentals. When doctors commit to pursuing health and wholeness in ways that help and don't harm patients, they begin to achieve a practice of medicine befitting a "good doctor" – a practice that realizes medicine's internal goods, a practice that benefits all. ⟶

4. Alasdair MacIntyre, *After Virtue* (Notre Dame, IN: Notre Dame Univ. Press:2010): 187.
5. Cavanaugh, *Hippocrates' Oath*, 124–30.

Chaim Bezalel and Yonnah Ben Levy, *Rimonim*, mixed media on encaustic

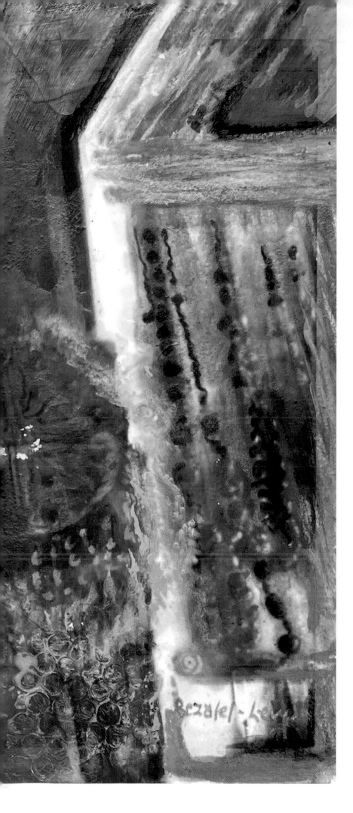

The
Dance of
Devotion

*Lifestyle discipline in
achievers is admired.
Religious discipline in
believers, not so much.*

KELSEY OSGOOD

*C*ONFESSION: I am a *little* obsessed with cloistered contemplative nuns. It's gotten to the point at which my YouTube algorithm is giving me nothing but interviews with women about their vocation stories, or short documentaries that offer a glimpse into the serene environs of Carmelite or Poor Clare monasteries: sisters picking apples, chanting, lying completely prostrate on the floor during professions of vows. Years ago, a friend gave me a book about the daily routines of famous writers and thinkers – W. H. Auden rose at six sharp and disdained working at night; Willa Cather wrote for three hours a day, max – but today I am more interested in the highly regimented schedules of these hidden women. Sometimes I idly wonder if I could rise in the middle of the night to pray, glutton for sleep that I am, or if I'd succumb to the urge to chat before evening recreation time (the answer is almost certainly yes).

This is a very unorthodox fixation for me, an Orthodox Jew. After all, my own life is rife with examples of religious discipline, even if it often feels more frenetic than the kind exhibited by the nuns. For example, I began writing this essay during the height of Pesach preparations. Most people know that on Passover, Jews do not eat bread or other leavened products, but considerably fewer know how intense and detailed the purgative lead-up to Pesach can be for the traditionally observant. Every inch of my kitchen is thoroughly cleaned; plates and cutlery are replaced by alternates whose surfaces have never been besmirched by breadcrumbs; not just cereal and bagels but mustard, sesame seeds, and couscous are packed into closed closets or donated, and I'm one of the lazier Pesach *balabustas* out there. On my synagogue's WhatsApp group chat, congregants ask the kinds of questions that to outsiders must look like angels-dancing-on-a-pin stuff: Can I keep my Brita water filter on my faucet through the holiday? Can I use white vinegar to remove smells from laundry? Can I drink milk without specific Pesach kosher certification? (Answers: yes, no, and only if you buy it before the holiday starts.)

I'm accustomed to people finding the demands of Jewish ritual life nonsensical, but I admit to being a little confused when I can't immediately sell others on the beauty of cloistered living. I thought the appeal of retreat would be obvious, considering how much people complain about how uniquely terrible modern life is. When I chew someone's ear off about the Poor Clares, the most common response I get is, "But wouldn't these people be more effective out in the world?" This is a curious contemporary deontology,

---

Kelsey Osgood is the author of How to Disappear Completely: On Modern Anorexia *and has written for the* New York Times, *the* New Yorker, Longreads, *and the* Washington Post. *She is working on a book about religious conversion for Viking Penguin.*

to imply that participating in society is an inherent good regardless of its outcome. (Is a publicist inherently virtuous for "contributing"? An advertising executive? A real estate developer?) The only retort that invariably works is, "But their carbon footprints must be nearly zero!" What I have to do, it seems, is translate the cloistered life into the language of modern heroics.

The average modern person's reaction to the idea of cloistered vocation reveals a great deal, actually, about our current attitudes toward obligation, sacrifice, and discipline. Asked to define the final term, most people immediately identify two distinct strands: the power of a person to give up or abstain from something, and the wherewithal required to stick to a demanding schedule or maintain a singular focus in order to reach the highest echelons of achievement. So let's call these "abstention discipline" and "lifestyle discipline."

Generally speaking, lifestyle discipline is more likely to garner respect. This is most evident in fields that involve performing for an audience, such as sports, dance, or music. (Exceptional visual art and writing might also provoke awe, but because they're done in private, it's usually of a quieter, delayed variety.) Think of our reverence as we watch a particularly gifted violin virtuoso perform or a skating prodigy seemingly float above the ice. The awe is often heightened by the thought of the sacrifices that must have been required to reach

this apex. "This young lady has been dreaming of the Olympics since she was four years old!" breathless announcers inform the rapt crowd. We assume that the person had to engage in all manner of abstention discipline to excel – think of all the birthday cake forgone by the budding Olympian, or the hours practicing scales when one's school pals were playing outdoors – but

We live in an age that glorifies self-care to the point of parody, whereby any attempt to deny oneself something pleasurable is suspect.

because it's done in service of a goal that contains some element of the transcendent, it's seen as worth it. Perhaps we recognize in this striving an outsized version of a satisfaction we have all experienced in miniature, as psychologists suggest that humans find the most meaning in projects that involve some hardship.

Outside of performance, stories involving serious lifestyle discipline evoke slightly more ambivalent reactions: people remain deeply attracted to them, but dissenting voices often arise, asking, as people did regarding the nuns, what exactly the *point* of it is, or whether it's worth whatever is produced in the end. In 2011, throngs of people flocked to see *Jiro Dreams of Sushi,* a documentary about Jiro Ono, a Japanese sushi chef so devoted to his craft that his tiny restaurant, located in a subway station, received a three-star Michelin rating. Ono was so exacting in his demands that employees weren't permitted to prepare food until they'd learned the proper way to squeeze the hand towels offered to guests upon arrival, which could take weeks or even years; when an apprentice finally made a passable *tamago*

Photograph by alefbet26. Used by permission.

Chaim Bezalel
and Yonnah Ben
Levy, *Magilla*,
mixed media
on cotton rag
paper, 2006

omelet, he wept with joy. Audiences arrived in droves, but critics were torn about Ono's single-mindedness. "This is a portrait of tunnel vision," the critic Roger Ebert wrote – he didn't mean it as a compliment – noting that Ono's relationship to a meal that can be consumed in a matter of minutes "wavers between love and madness." And when a pursuit is full of hazard, that changes the calculus for some. "I just can't get behind calling this incredibly risky behavior a sport, and I don't want to aid in its glorification," said a review of the documentary *Free Solo*, which chronicles Alex Honnold's attempt to climb the face of El Capitan without safety equipment. Sure, ascending 3,000 feet up a sheet of rock, with the possibility of death at any moment, is an impressive, even majestic, feat. But what about this man's family? Or the film crew, who would live with the image of his demise for the rest of their lives if so much as a single digit slipped?

Is he any different from an adrenaline seeker we'd be more immediately suspicious of, like a street racer or a drug addict?

In contrast, abstention discipline tends to garner a more universally negative reaction. This plays out a lot regarding diet. Dietary restrictions have always existed, of course, but in the past two decades, the number of ways in which you can restrict your diet, and the reasons you might cite for doing so, have exploded. You can be on a low-FODMAP plan for your irritable bowels, or eschew nightshades because you're Gisele Bündchen, or be vegan because of the environment, or be gluten-free for a real malady or gluten-free because of an imaginary malady: the list stretches on. But even those who've taken undeniably ethical paths, like abstaining from animal products for reasons of animal rights or the environment, are often perceived as smug, judgmental, or self-involved. Part of this is that we live in an age that glorifies self-care to the point of parody, whereby any attempt to deny yourself something pleasurable is suspect, unless you're engaged in the limited kinds of lifestyle discipline we easily venerate (the aforementioned music, dance, and athletics). Another reason is that we often take the choices of others as a direct commentary on our own: we feel implicitly judged for tucking into a hamburger while our dining companion seems satisfied with rice and beans. In my own life, I've recently begun to tell friends that I hope to give up air travel at some point in the not-too-distant future, and nearly all of them have responded by telling me that the planes are still going to fly even if I don't buy a ticket, or that personal travel only accounts for some vanishingly small percentage of carbon released into the atmosphere, or that it shouldn't be the responsibility of individuals to counteract the harm that is done by a handful of behemoth corporations. Their defenses are generic – and not entirely wrong – but it's clear to me that they're also deeply personal: if they accepted that my choice was the morally correct one, they would have to change their own travel habits, and they (understandably) don't want to. (Lest this seem extra holy on my part, rest assured I've rolled my eyes at plenty of vegans in my day.)

Religious discipline confounds the modern sensibility because it upends our ideas about the value of discipline and sacrifice. To a person steeped in modern heroics, religious discipline looks solely like abstention, with none of the benefits of lifestyle discipline. It is giving up pleasurable things just to make your life less enjoyable; it is overcoming, ignoring, or dismissing your own desires solely from masochism, or because of communal expectations, which is the worst possible sin these days, to do something because someone or some group expects you to. (Contrast this with the Talmudic discussion of whether it is better to perform an action because you're commanded to or because you want to, which rules firmly on the side of commandment: "Greater is one who is commanded to do a mitzvah and performs it than one who is not commanded to do a mitzvah and performs it.") People often disdain the religious because they feel the

What if a life of faith is itself a kind of creative pursuit, an athletics of the soul?

religious expect them, too, to give up the things they enjoy. (Sometimes we do, but not as often as people assume.) And faith pervades every aspect of our lives, but we can't monetize it or craft "peak experiences" out of it. There's not going to be the satisfaction of a finish line even if it's a sort of marathon. It is production with no product, a project with no deadline, a rock face with no summit.

But what if, instead, people saw all our pesky obligatory rituals, and all the stuff that looks like deprivation for deprivation's sake, not as a program of self-torture but as a technology by which we allow ourselves to refine a certain set of skills? What if a life of faith is itself a kind of creative pursuit, or an athletics of the soul? "It's like a beautiful old cathedral or an old building," a cloistered Poor Clare told the writer Abbie Reese for her book *Dedicated to God: An Oral History of Cloistered Nuns*. "The *life* is a work of art, this eight-hundred-year-old order." This is the thesis of the Stanford anthropologist T. M. Luhrmann, who has written prolifically about religious ritual and its effects on believers. After careful observation in environs as different as synagogues for newly Orthodox Jews in California and charismatic churches in Ghana, Luhrmann posited that the behavioral structures of religions are not in place only as a means of worshiping God, but also as a way of shaping the human beings themselves, by making them more open to mystical experiences, more oriented toward gratitude, more meticulous about small, detailed actions like the kind involved in ritualistic behaviors, and better able to enter a state of pure attention (she calls this "absorption"), among other things. "In fact, when you look carefully, you can see that

> *We dance on the heads of pins, and maybe few people see or care, but it's the most exquisite ballet you'll never see.*

church is about changing people's mental habits Sunday by Sunday so that they feel that God is more real, more relevant, and more present for them," Luhrmann writes in *How God Becomes Real: Kindling the Presence of Invisible Others.*

In the course of working on a book about religious conversion, I've met many people who have given up all manner of things in service of their newfound beliefs: driving, television, alcohol, meat, social media, the ability to leave their place of residence whenever they want, zippers, coffee, health insurance, property ownership, footwear, pork, sex, marriage. They've made public and private promises never to partake not only of luxuries, but of the kinds of things most people, certainly most Americans, consider essential. These choices are not random acts of self-denial. Often they bind the person practically to a faith community: an Amish convert I recently spent time with said she obviously understood a car would be more convenient than a buggy, but it would give people the ability to travel further outside their area on a more regular basis, and

thus fracture the strong ties they shared with one another. Sometimes, in the case of nuns or monks, the sacrifices are made in an attempt to strip away worldly distractions to allow them to more readily enter the meditative state required for prayer.

When you subtract the religious element of some of these choices, they make evident sense to even a secular observer. Abstaining from alcohol, under the clever new label "sober curious," has been massively trending for the past few years, and among the benefits people cite, maintaining clearer cognition ranks highly. A person who gives up alcohol is still likely to be judged by others as uptight, but less than the Mormon or Muslim who doesn't drink for religious reasons, even though maintaining a clear mind is part of the reason for the ordinance in both faiths.

Much religious discipline does involve a measure of bodily denial, in the case of alcohol, food, or sex. For some, that isn't wholly pleasant. I do not enjoy keeping kosher all that much, actually. I don't miss the cheeseburgers or lobsters of my youth at all, and I enjoy thinking of skipping these as a potential opportunity for holiness, but I absolutely *hate* how often I have to turn down food when I'm visiting others (no matter how many caveats I offer, it never fails to come across as rude) or how difficult it makes traveling. The difficulty, it turns out, is rather by design. In a Midrashic commentary on the book of *Vayikra*, Rabbi Elazar ben Azaryah is quoted as saying, "Whence is it derived that a man should not say: I do not desire to wear [linen and wool]; I do not desire to eat the flesh of a pig; I do not desire to cohabit with [improper sexual relationships]. I do desire it, but what can I do? My Father in heaven has decreed against it!" The twinge that comes with renunciation – so deeply alien a concept, let alone a *value*, to twenty-first-century morality – helps us craft

our bodies as well as our lives into vessels for holiness.

Just as becoming an elite athlete requires both an intense physical regimen and the ability to maintain psychological focus, a life of religious devotion requires practices of renunciation to hone our physical, mental, and spiritual muscles, as well as attention to the mind and the body and the delicate interplay between them. The comparison becomes even more apt when you look at the kind of language athletes use to describe the way they feel at peak performance. "The body, by force of the soul, can in fact be converted into a luminous fluid. . . . When, in its divine power, it completely possesses the body, it converts that into a luminous moving cloud and thus can manifest itself in the whole of its divinity." This statement wouldn't be out of place in the writings of a mystic like Hildegard of Bingen. But no: it comes from the modern-dance luminary Isadora Duncan's memoir.

When a dancer performs "Blue Danube" with Duncan's choreography, onlookers may watch, breathless, feeling certain that they're witnessing a work of near-divine beauty. They can sense some kind of greatness at work – greatness both of body and of spirit – and feel grateful that others have toiled to realize it for their consumption. Some may wish to try to mimic this experience in their own lives, by running marathons or swimming great distances or going on arduous hikes; they might even recognize that some of what satisfies them about doing so is directly related to the mental and physical hardship involved, about feeling it and enduring it and then moving beyond it.

Religion, even, can attract this kind of discomfort tourism: think of the people who sign up to do ten-day silent retreats at Zen centers, or who apply to live for a short time with an Amish family, or who pay to dunk in a ritual mikvah in hopes of manufacturing some kind of spiritual experience, or because they have some kind of vague sense that emotionally charged moments should be marked in a way that is sacred but they have no idea how to do that in a culture bereft of such opportunities. Personally, I am skeptical that these small bursts of discipline have the long-lasting salutary benefits people seek. They may help clear your mind or refine your spirit or strengthen your body in the short term. But once you go back to your default state you would have to redo the exercise just to reach that same level, as it would be if a musician ceased to practice daily and then tried to perform Paganini on the spot.

The elite athlete and the perfected mystic must not only dabble in discipline, not only praise it, to paraphrase a Cervantes quote, but submit to it. And while achievement in the realms of spirituality and performance are reached via remarkably similar disciplined paths, only the performative is met with ovation. Maybe that's fine, because acclaim isn't at all the point. For some, public acclaim is itself the thing to abstain from; avoiding it becomes, as it does for the cloistered, its own kind of discipline, another way in which religious values stand in opposition to the moral lodestars of our time. The invisible devotees among us, whether the Poor Clares or the bedraggled Jewish women of the Bronx: we dance on the heads of pins, and maybe few people see or care, but it's the most exquisite ballet you'll never see. ➤

Masterpiece of Impossibility

CAITRIN KEIPER

In Victor Hugo's *Les Misérables*,
competing vows reveal the paradox of grace.

I T IS THE ONLY LIE the holy bishop has ever told. Yes, he assures the police who come to him with a desperate convict and a fabulous story, he *did* give Jean Valjean the silver he was found with, the silver everyone there knows perfectly well that Valjean stole. In fact, he adds to Valjean, thinking quickly, here are two candlesticks (his only prized possessions); "would you leave the best behind?" he sings in the musical version of Victor Hugo's *Les Misérables*.

Having thus cemented the story and convinced the police to go away, the bishop makes his true purpose known: "But remember this, my brother. See in this some higher plan. You must use this precious silver to become an honest man," he continues. "God has raised you out of darkness. I have bought your soul for God." Even as he sings of raising up, his voice descends to the deep, as if reenacting Christ's harrowing of hell for one poor soul.

The one poor soul stands reeling as the turntable (a central feature of the original stage set) whisks the bishop away. Alone, Valjean confronts what he was and thought he knew – "For I had come to hate the world. The world that always hated me!" – and this new revelation: "He told me that I have a soul.

How does he know? What spirit comes to move my life? Is there another way to go?" Toppled off his axis, he trembles:

> I am reaching, but I fall,
> And the night is closing in,
> And I stare into the void,
> To the whirlpool of my sin.

But instead of plunging in, he is caught by mercy and flung back up toward God. This conversion propels the rest of the action. As Valjean, he disappears, and under new names he devotes his life to others. He rebuilds a struggling town, gives many alms, saves an injured man, shows compassion to a friendless woman, rescues her young child. Most of these acts are at least somewhat joyful or gratifying, but then there are the others where he must die to self: he gives himself up for a man mistaken for him who is being sent back to prison in his place; he endangers his own life to protect the man his daughter loves, the one who will take her away from him; he frees the man who has been hunting him and volunteers to be arrested.

As the turntable spins, the cycles of misery and oppression yielding endless iterations, while the revolution meant to break out of them revolves back on itself, the true

Opposite:
Hugh Jackman as Jean Valjean in the 2012 film version of *Les Misérables* directed by Tom Hooper

---

Caitrin Keiper is editor-at-large of Plough *and a senior editor of the* New Atlantis. *She lives in Virginia.*

PictureLux / The Hollywood Archive / Alamy Stock Photo. Used by permission.

Hugh Jackman as Jean Valjean (2012 film)

forward motion comes from this moment when a soul at one still point in time makes contact with eternity.

In the book, this is not what happens.

IN THE BOOK, after the bishop pardons him, the first thing Valjean does as a free man is, pointlessly, another crime. Troubled but not yet transformed, and now in possession of more wealth than he ever saw in his life, he nabs a coin from a little boy scampering in the forest. The boy pleads for it back while Valjean stands there and glowers. Eventually he scares the boy away. Belatedly overwhelmed by what he's done, he tries to run after the boy to make it right, but cannot find him. *Then* he has his crisis of conscience. Kneeling unseen outside the bishop's door, he embraces a redemption that cost him nothing but will ask of him everything.

What must the bishop think when he learns what has happened? Everyone would soon hear of the boy robbed by a stranger; no one could know of Valjean's repentance and his hidden life of service. From this point, the detective Javert will begin to track him from one secret identity to the next, convinced his life of crime must be ongoing – and as far as the bishop can know for sure, this isn't wrong. If the bishop were forced to put together such a thing as a philanthropic impact statement, he would have to report the waste of his resources on a recidivist. The sister and the housekeeper who live with him, suspicious from the start, will surely take every opportunity to say they told him so. "For a long time I have wrongfully been withholding this silver. It belonged to the poor. Who was this man? A poor man, quite clearly," he placidly explained to them after the initial theft was discovered; but now, after this generous second chance? After Valjean betrays his "promise"?

The promise, as the book describes it, was made prior to his own knowledge of it: "Do not forget, ever, that you have promised me to use this silver to become an honest man," the bishop said. "Jean Valjean, who had no recollection of any such promise, stood dumbfounded," writes Hugo. It seems the bishop has somehow vowed this on Valjean's behalf, which is impossible. But in that very impossibility lies the reason why all this is irrelevant to the grace the bishop has offered, and even why the outcome is not his to know.

The vicarious vow in the book is one step further than the simple command to go and sin no more of the musical, but in both versions, the bishop elaborates on this transaction with the language of a purchase, speaking of "buying" Valjean's soul: "I withdraw it from dark thoughts and the spirit of perdition, and I give it to God," he says in the book. This purchase can *only* be vicarious, for souls cannot be paid for from their own bankrupt accounts. The debt that this creates cannot be repaid to the creditor, but must be satisfied another way.

In the Parable of the Unmerciful Servant (Matt. 18:21–35), a man is forgiven a great sum by his master, but for a small debt owed in turn to him, he throws the debtor into prison. The master hauls him up and asks why he could not show the same mercy that was shown to him. This is the only requirement that mercy has. The bishop knows he is just another sinner whose soul was once paid for too. What can he do but extend the same to Valjean? It is a contract with grace, a gift that demands only that it be re-given.

Rather than a voluntary and symmetrical arrangement between two parties, the contract with grace is a line pointing onward, stretching to infinity as it is passed on from one person to the next. It is not binding so much as it is liberating; unbound from "dark thoughts and the spirit of perdition," Valjean has the freedom to do anything, even reject it (as someone later will). But as long as Valjean proceeds within this line of grace, and after he embraces the vow himself in his conversion, it invisibly supports him. Having always been noted for his supreme physical strength, he finds a matching spiritual strength to do what's right, and make impossible self-sacrifices when they're called for. "My soul belongs to God, I know, I made that bargain long ago. He gave me hope when hope was gone, he gave me strength to journey on," he recalls at one anguished moment in the musical, mustering his will to match his conscience.

In the book, after the bishop dies (and presumably is glad to finally learn the truth), Valjean often draws inspiration from the sense that he is looking down on him, "that men could see his mask, but the bishop saw his face." In life as in death, the bishop is the only one who ever really saw his face at all, from which others "would have erased from that existence the word that the finger of God has nonetheless written on the brow of everyone – *Hope!*"

"Everyone" includes a character perhaps even less likely than Valjean to be imprinted with this

Russell Crowe as Javert (2012 film)

word, someone whose spiritual capacity seems to fall well outside it. Someone who doesn't even have a Christian name but only the surname Javert. Someone who must be the least, and therefore most, likely person Valjean would be expected to confront with grace.

"There is a way of avoiding a person that resembles a search," Hugo observes in the book.

> The contract with grace is a line pointing onward, stretching to infinity as it is passed on from one person to the next.

As the June Rebellion of 1832 takes shape in the streets of Paris, Valjean and Javert catch up to each other at the barricades, where Valjean has stationed himself to help his daughter's lover, Marius, and Javert has gone undercover to spy on the revolutionaries. When Javert is found out and sentenced to death by their leader, Enjolras, Valjean takes the opportunity to settle several debts at once. For Enjolras's debt of gratitude to

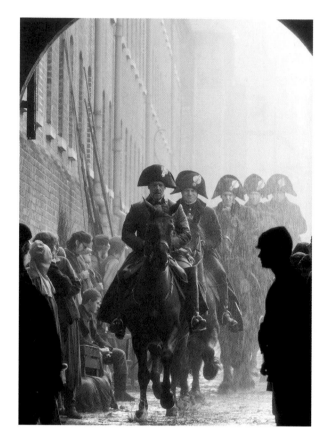

plane where order is maintained, a civilization churning along atop its filthy sewers. In the musical, Javert sings in perfect fourths and fifths, fixed intervals with no possibility of modulation. He believes in a truth as firm and absolute as stars, "filling the darkness with order and light." And like the stars above, Javert's commitment to this ideal transcends his own interests: at one point in the book he turns himself in for an infraction against his vow to the law: "In my life I have often been severe toward others. It was just. I was right. Now if I were not severe toward myself, all I have justly done would have become injustice. Should I spare myself more than others? No. You see! If I had been eager only to punish others and not myself, that would have been despicable! . . . Good God, it is easy to be kind, the difficulty is to be just."

That is the difficulty indeed. As noble causes go, the law would be a fine one, if the law were just. "Do not think that I have come to abolish the law," said Jesus; "I have come not to abolish but to fulfill" (Matt. 5:17). But Javert's target is not Thénardier but Valjean, his law itself inflicts injustice, and Jesus' version of fulfillment is the very thing he cannot stand. When Valjean's pardon gives him a glimpse of it, he is aghast. Writes Hugo:

> Javert had never seen the unknown except below. The irregular, the unexpected, the disorderly opening of chaos, the possible slipping into an abyss; all of that belonged to inferior regions, to the rebellious, the wicked, the miserable. Now Javert was thrown over backward, and he was startled by this monstrous apparition: a gulf above him.

him for his valor and protection in the battle, he secures custody of Javert; for his debt to the law that he broke long ago, he surrenders his address and future liberty; and for Javert's debt to him, for hounding him throughout his life and undoing any hope of earthly happiness, Valjean "takes his revenge" and undoes Javert himself. Laying his life at Javert's feet, Valjean lets him walk free.

A WORD IN DEFENSE of our villain, the indefatigable Inspector Javert. His character in both the book and the musical is defined by the law, a law meant to control the vice and disorder spread by such people as the con man Thénardier and his cronies, and even Javert's own parents. He considers himself as having crawled up from the mire of sin into which he was born onto a

Reeling at the possibility that goodness is as fathomless as evil, Javert stares "into the void of a world that cannot hold," as he sings in the musical's reprise of Valjean's conversion song. Of one thing he remains certain:

> I am the law and the law is not mocked!
> I'll spit his pity right back in his face.
> There is nothing on earth that we share:
> It is either Valjean or Javert!

But of course there is everything that they share, even the syllables of their names in reverse. Each has spent his life in relation to the other. Each is bound to a principle greater than himself. Each of them, like the bishop, like the unmerciful servant, like anyone, is a sinner in need of grace.

Javert does not want it. The contract ends with him. And yet.

As with Valjean's encounter with grace before it, there is one little detail that complicates this event. Just as when Valjean is sent forth to a new life and instead steals a coin, he does "a thing of which he was no longer capable," Javert now does something of which he was not capable before. When they meet again outside the barricades, Javert moves to arrest Valjean but ultimately lets him go. Javert, who "would have arrested his own father if he escaped from prison and turned in his own mother for breaking parole," cannot bring himself to punish the man *he* now owes a debt of life. As Hugo writes, "to sacrifice duty, that general obligation, to personal motives, and to feel in these motives something general too, and perhaps superior," goes against everything in him, but that is what he does.

It seems that Javert also has a living soul of which he had been unaware. But rather than reckon with what it is trying to tell him or reconcile the paradox of it all, Javert chooses annihilation. He looks into the face of mercy and then jumps into the Seine.

Meanwhile, Valjean, whose forgiveness of Javert cost him more dearly than the bishop's gift of candlesticks did him, does not know what comes of it either, and spends the final stretch of his life expecting an arrest at any time. This act of grace, even more so than the bishop's, might truly seem to be a waste. At least, the meaning is obscure. But like Christ's own grace, not universally accepted but freely given from one moment into all of time, it is offered in faith that it is not meaningless.

MUCH OF WHAT HAPPENS in *Les Misérables* seems, in the immediate sense, just as futile. The revolution is an abject failure. Its leaders give their lives for nothing. The world turns, the cycle repeats, "round and round and back where you began," as the surviving witnesses to the revolution sing in resignation.

When the book was first published in 1862, poet and politician Alphonse de Lamartine

---

> ## As noble causes go, the law would be a fine one, if the law were just.

---

criticized it as a "masterpiece of impossibility" and a "dangerous" story, "because everything is impossible in the aspirations of *Les Misérables*, and the main impossibility is that all our suffering will disappear." But for whom among the miserables does suffering disappear? Rather, the book hit a nerve in this frustrated former progressive. Bitterly, he said, "If we sow ideal and impossible thoughts in the masses, we reap the sacred fury of their disillusionment," evidently speaking for himself.

According to Hugo, the answer to such disillusionment lies above us:

Photo 12 / Alamy Stock Photo. Used by permission.

Shall we continue to look upwards? Is the light we can see in the sky one of those that will presently be extinguished? The ideal is terrifying to behold, lost as it is in the depths, small, isolated, a pin-point, brilliant but threatened on all sides by the dark forces that surround it: nevertheless, no more in danger than a star in the jaws of the clouds.

The stars that Javert swore by, and yet was so astonished to witness in the gulf above him, the stars that illumined Valjean's vow made at the beginning and Javert's vow broken at the end, are a promise made by heaven, immovable in the firmament. But still they are distant, and often obscured.

Contra Lamartine, the main impossibility in the ideal of *Les Misérables* is not that suffering will disappear, but that it can be redeemed; that brokenness does not erase the hope in any person; that dormant souls come back to life; that the cycle of retribution breaks for grace. And for symbolic confirmation of this impossible reality, there is an intimation of the stars on earth – that is, candles.

Valjean treasures the bishop's candlesticks for his entire life. Their candlelight shines upon his face as he dies. Such little stars on earth have a secret power even the stars above do not: they can ignite each other, one to the next to the next ad infinitum, without losing their own light. So Jean Valjean, entrusted with his candlesticks, carried them through life and lit the way for others; and coming finally to rest, he passed the flame. ⬿

The One Who Promises

We can only make vows because Another is faithful.

KING-HO LEUNG

THE MAKING, KEEPING, AND BREAKING of promises, oaths, and vows seems to be something close to Taylor Swift's heart. On the title track of her 2010 album *Speak Now*, Swift sings of a girl "rudely barging in on a white veil occasion" to deliver a message to the boy that she loves who is about to marry someone else: "Don't wait or say a single *vow*; you need to hear me out, and they said 'speak now.'" Or there is the memorable line in one of her best-loved songs, "All Too Well" (2012): "You call me up again just to break me like a *promise*, so casually cruel in the name of being honest." Nearly a decade later, Swift released a ten-minute version of "All Too Well" (2021) with expanded lyrics and an accompanying music video that sparked global gossip about who the subject of Swift's jilted fury could be. In contrast to her lover's flippant promise-breaking, Swift expresses her own devotion: "You kept me like a secret, but I kept you like an *oath* – sacred prayer and we'd swear to remember it – all too well."

Swift's lyrics prompt questions that have plagued thinkers down the ages, stretching from Thomas Aquinas to Martin Luther to Giorgio Agamben, from ancient philosophers to the earliest stories in the Hebrew scriptures:

What difference does a promise really make? Will something have changed once the love of Swift's life has said the "single vow" she begs him not to? Is there a connection between an oath and what Swift calls a "sacred prayer"? Many thinkers through history have argued that the invocation of God is an essential aspect of swearing oaths and making vows. While many no longer believe in God, people – not least Taylor Swift – still seem to be drawn to believing in the power of vows, oaths, and promises almost as if there is still a God who listens to the vows we make.

The connection between the divine and the human practice of making promises lies at the heart of the contemporary Italian philosopher Giorgio Agamben's 2008 book *The Sacrament of Language: An Archaeology of the Oath*. Agamben notes that "one of the characteristics of the oath on which all the authorities, both ancient and modern, from Cicero to Glotz, from Augustine to Benveniste, seem to be in agreement is the calling of the gods as witnesses." Among the various accounts of the oath in the history of Western philosophy, Agamben pays specific attention to the Hellenistic Jewish philosopher Philo of Alexandria (ca. 20 BC–ca. AD 50),

---

King-Ho Leung is Senior Research Fellow at St Mary's College, University of St Andrews, where he currently co-directs the research initiative Widening Horizons in Philosophical Theology.

who in his work *Legum allegoriae* discusses the oath which God makes to Abraham in Genesis 22:16–17. This oath comes as a dramatic resolution to the scene after Abraham promises God to sacrifice his only son Isaac. Having spared Isaac at the last moment, God provides a ram to be sacrificed in Isaac's stead and fulfills Abraham's promise for him. It is shortly after this moment that God makes an oath to Abraham, saying: "By myself I have sworn."

Commenting on God's declaration, Philo considers whether it is appropriate to say that God is one who can swear an oath:

> Some have said, that it was inappropriate for Him to swear; for an oath is added to assist faith [*pisteōs eneka*] and only God . . . is faithful [*pistos*] . . . They say indeed that an oath is calling God to witness [*martyria*] to a point which is disputed; so if it is God that swears, He bears witness to Himself, which is absurd, for he that bears the witness must be a different person from him on whose behalf it is borne.

Contrary to this position, Philo argues that because God is the highest and best of all things, God cannot swear by any other thing – for there is nothing higher or better than God – but only by himself: "God alone therefore is the strongest security first for Himself, and in the next place for his deeds also, so that He naturally swore by Himself when giving assurance as to himself, a thing impossible for anyone but God."

Philo's insistence that God cannot swear by anything higher than himself not only anticipates the New Testament teaching in Hebrews 6:13 that "when God made a promise to Abraham, because he had no one greater by whom to swear, he swore by himself," but also coincides with Jesus Christ's teaching in Matthew 5:34–35: "Do not swear at all, either by heaven, for it is the throne of God, or by the earth, for it is his footstool, or by Jerusalem,

for it is the city of the great King." The Church Father and Bible translator Jerome (ca. 342–420) comments on Matthew 5:34: "The Savior here has not prohibited swearing by God, but by heaven and earth and Jerusalem." While Quakers and Anabaptists would later question this interpretation and argue that Jesus unequivocally renounces the swearing of oaths in this passage, what Jerome's fourth-century interpretation highlights is the *transcendent* nature of God: for Jerome, as for Jesus' contemporary Philo, humans should not swear by heaven or by earth or by Jerusalem, because all these things are but creations and possessions of God – his "throne," his "footstool," his "city" – which are lower and lesser beings than God. As Hebrews 6:16–17 puts it, "humans swear by someone greater than themselves," someone whose purpose and faithfulness – and indeed whose promises – are "unchangeable": namely, God.

This, however, presents a conundrum for Philo: though God is the only fitting assurance for humans to swear by, how can human beings swear by God whose transcendent nature is incomprehensible to them? Writing in the first-century context of Hellenistic Judaism – which, unlike Christianity, did not believe that the divine nature is made known to humanity through Christ's incarnation – Philo argues that it is improper for human creatures to swear by God, for only God alone has full knowledge of his own nature and essence – something which can never be comprehended by creaturely beings: humans would not know what they are invoking if they swear by God who is ineffable in his divine nature. In his reading of Genesis 22:16, Philo therefore insists that only God can swear by himself: all other creatures do not and cannot swear "by God" but rather "by God's *name*." According to Philo, since finite human creatures do not and cannot grasp the infinite transcendent nature of God, they can only swear by God's *name* – the name which has

Yoram Raanan,
Between Us, oil
on canvas, 1986

been generously revealed and given to them by God, which allows humans to call upon God in an intimate and personal manner. Philo connects this insight to Moses' teaching in Deuteronomy:

> Naturally no one swears by Him, since he is unable to possess knowledge regarding His nature. No, we may be content if we are able to swear by his name . . . Moses, too, let us observe, filled with wonder at the transcendency of the Uncreated, says, "And thou shalt swear by His Name" (Deut. 6:13), not "by Him," for it is enough for the created being that he should be accredited and have witness borne to him by the Divine word. . . . The very words of God are oaths.

As finite created beings, human beings can only make oaths because God has revealed himself to them in the form of a word (*logos*) – what Philo calls "the Divine word" – that is his name. Human beings can swear oaths in God's name only because God has revealed his name to them. In this sense, Taylor Swift is right to draw a connection between oaths and "sacred prayers": in giving us his name, God made a way for us to address our oaths to him directly, personally, even prayerfully. But what about vows? Is a vow different from an oath? If so, what is God's involvement with a vow?

Writing some twelve centuries after Philo and Jesus, the medieval Dominican scholastic Thomas Aquinas (1225–74) makes a technical distinction between oaths and vows in his *Summa Theologiae*:

> A vow binds one to God while an oath sometimes binds one to man. . . . The obligation both of a vow and of an oath arises from something Divine; but in different ways. For the obligation of a vow arises from the fidelity we owe God, which binds us to fulfil our promises to Him. On the other hand, the obligation of an oath arises from the reverence we owe Him which binds us to make true what we promise in His name. (II–II.89.8)

According to Aquinas, where the obligations of vows express our fidelity to God, the obligations of our oaths reflect our reverence toward God. With the increasing popularity and influence of religious orders such as the Franciscans and the Dominicans (founded respectively in 1209 and 1216), the distinction between vows and oaths was quite important, including for Aquinas, who would have made a vow when he joined the Dominican order. To make a vow and dedicate one's life to God – as those who join religious orders do – is understood as categorically different from the swearing of oaths, which need not necessarily pertain to anything religious. After all, unlike a vow which is a promise made to God, an oath is not a promise one makes to God but merely to fellow human beings.

It was precisely this emphasis on promises made to God through vow-taking which would trouble many of the Reformers just a few centuries later. In 1505, Martin Luther left university, sold all his books, and entered the St. Augustine's Monastery in Erfurt. As per the practice of his time, Luther would have taken the three monastic vows of obedience, poverty, and chastity upon entering the religious life. However, the monastic vows Luther took did not give him the spiritual life and peace that he wanted. Instead, his attempts to adhere to the promises he made only brought him spiritual distress and existential crises. Less than two decades later, Luther would present fierce theological critiques of the culture and spiritual implications of taking monastic vows in his 1521 work *De Votis Monasticis*. Luther worried that such promises to God could be seen as binding or forcing one to perform actions or indeed works for God, which would be directly in tension with what he saw as the biblical teaching of justification by faith and not by works. Luther writes:

> [God] gave you the freedom in all things and made you free. What else is a vow except your making something obligatory that he declares is a matter of choice. But in granting you this freedom God does not prevent you from putting yourself under obligation or binding yourself to your neighbor, because your neighbor has not, like God, commanded you to be free.

The binding character of a monastic vow as a promise made to God was, in Luther's eyes, too law-like, as if the vow were a kind of crypto-contract or legal agreement between God and the human vower that compromised the freedom and gift of salvation God freely gives to the human believer through faith. While it may seem that Luther calls us to not "say a single vow" (to invoke Swift's lyrics), Luther was mainly concerned with monastic and religious vows, as opposed to the marriage vows that Taylor Swift sang of, because for Luther marriage vows (or, perhaps more accurately, marriage oaths) are effectively binding promises made to another person with God as witness, rather than promises made to God.

In his critique of religious vows, Luther sought to emphasize that God's salvation is a free gift for the Christian believer; in his view, the human fulfillment of their obligations or promises to God is ultimately unattainable. Instead, for Luther, the relationship between God and creature is not the outworking of any human effort or fulfillments of human promises made to God. Rather, it is an outworking of God's divine promise to his creatures. He writes in *De Libertate Christiana* (1520):

> What is impossible for you, by means of all the works of the commandments, which are many, and which still cannot be of any value, is made simple and easy for you through faith. For God has made all things depend on faith, so that whoever has it shall have all things and be joyful; whoever does not have it shall have nothing. This is what the promises of God provide, what the commandments demand; they fulfill what the commandments demand, so that everything is from God himself, both commandment and fulfillment. He alone commands; he alone also fulfills.

Luther's famous doctrine of justification by faith is coupled with, or even premised on,

an emphasis on God's fulfillment of his own promise. For Luther, God's promise is made to us through the preaching of God's Word – or even God's divine act of giving us his Word.

Here we find different layers of meaning to God "giving his Word." On one level, God gives his Word to us as an act of communication or self-revelation (in the preaching of the "Word"). On a second level, God gives us his Word in the sense that his act of self-revelation is – always – an act of making a promise because, as Philo puts it, "the very words of God are oaths": God's Word is by definition faithful and trustworthy. On a third (or even trinitarian) level, one that goes beyond Philo's pre-Christian Hellenistic Judaism, one could say that God gave us his Word and made us a promise by giving us his Son, the one whom John's Gospel calls his Word: that God promises himself to us in the incarnate person of Jesus Christ. Understood in this distinctively Christian way, the faithful God who gives us his Word and fulfills his promise to us is a *trinitarian* God, for such a God is in his nature a *Word-giving* God in the sense that God is one who gives us his Word whom Christians call the second person of the Trinity. The very fact that God is one who faithfully keeps his promise is rooted in his character as a God who is always already – indeed eternally – giving his Word in his trinitarian nature.

From Philo to Aquinas to Luther we find insights not only into the nature of promises, but perhaps also into the nature of the God who reveals himself to his people in promises – or even *as* promise. God's nature as promise can be traced – beyond Luther, Aquinas, and even Philo – back to one of the most foundational moments in the Hebrew Bible: namely, God's self-revelation to Moses in Exodus 3. After the angel of the Lord appears to Moses in a burning bush, God reveals himself to Moses as the "God of your father, the God of Abraham, the God of Isaac, and the God of Jacob" (verse 6), calling to mind the oath God made to Abraham in the past. Honoring and fulfilling the promise he made to Abraham, God announces to Moses that he "has come down to deliver" his people from captivity into a promised land "flowing with milk and honey" (verse 8). God further promises that he will continue to be with Moses as he leads his people into future deliverance: "I will be with you" (verse 12). It is only then, when God's promises from past, present, and future have been rehearsed and assured that God reveals the Divine name: "I am who I am" or "I will be who I will be" (verse 14).

In the history of Western philosophy, the God who discloses his name as "I am who I am" or "I will be who I will be" in Exodus 3:14 is often understood to be "Being itself": "I *am* who I *am*" or "I will *be* who I will *be*" means that God is "Being" par excellence. According to this view, created beings only exist by participating in this God who is "Being itself" (cf. Acts 17:28). However, at the same time, God's very act of revealing and giving his name to his people can also be understood as an act of establishing some form of relationship with his people: a relationship which God promises to honor and uphold, because God is a faithful God – for "I will be who I will be" is not just a divine name but also a divine promise. Indeed, one might even say, God himself *is* promise – for God promises himself to his people in the very act of revealing his name to them. According to this reading, God is not simply an abstract philosophical principle of "Being" par excellence,

God is "faithfulness" or "promise" par excellence. God is not simply the idle object to whom one makes promises in vows, but also one who makes promises and always keeps them because he is faithful.

Unlike the disloyal human lover in Taylor Swift's "All Too Well," who is said to "call [her] up again just to break [her] like a promise," God is not someone who would ever break his promise. God's promise to us cannot be broken; it is intrinsically interwoven with our very being: for God called us into being by making a promise (Rom. 4:17). Just as created beings are said to exist by virtue of participating in the God who reveals himself to be "Being itself," creatures only have their being by virtue of God's promise to keep his Word and to continue sustaining the existence and integrity of his creation. In other words, to exist is to participate in God's promise: we only exist and have our creaturely being because God made us a promise and gave us his Word – by speaking the world into existence with and through his Word – through whom "all things came into being" (John 1:3), and in whom "all things hold together" (Col. 1:17). If, as Agamben would have it, "the word of God is, in the words of Philo, an oath," one can say that it is only because God first gave us his Word and made us a promise that we ourselves can make promises with our vows. Just as we love because God first loved us (1 John 4:19), it is because God first promised us that we can promise ourselves to God in vows. We can make vows and promises only because God first made us a promise, because God is the faithful one who keeps his promise, because God promised himself to us, because God gave us – and continues to give us – his Word. ⇝

Yuriy Khymych, *The Bell Tower of the Near and Far Caves (Kiev Lavra)*, 1993

Blessing the Bells

Bless the sounding bells—
The foundry and the furnace,
the partials and the pitch.

The cool bronze of their surface
cast out of molten metal—
a tolling out of reach.

The sheen of verdigris—
its pale protective touch.
The stony campanile

above us standing watch,
whose changes wake or warn us—
The fading fundamental,

like silence after speech,
forgotten as it trails
from each stroke over us—

spectral, subliminal—
waves breaking in the breach. . . .
Whose promise and what purpose

are carried by the bells
cast out of fire and furnace?
We bless each brazen pitch.

NED BALBO

Note: Plain Hunt Singles is a method of English full-circle ringing that requires three bells to be rung in a predetermined order ("ringing the changes"). Here, the rhymes are "rung" in the bell order of this method; the first and final stanzas' rhymes correspond to the order followed during rounds (repeatedly ringing the bells in sequence from the highest to lowest note).

A Vow
Will Keep You

RANDALL GAUGER

Artwork by Edmund Blair Leighton (public domain)

For a Bruderhof pastor, a lifelong vow makes
mutual faithfulness possible.

IF YOU LISTEN TO CHILDREN bickering, or adults for that matter, you will likely hear one party appeal to the other's sense of commitment: "But you promised! You gave me your word." Despite the fickleness of human nature, there seems to be an innate expectation that when people make a promise to do, or not do, something specific, they will hold to that promise. Someone who fails to do so is considered weak-willed or selfish.

A vow is a weightier promise, a solemn pledge dedicating oneself to an act, service, or way of life. Vows must be taken completely voluntarily and are spoken in the presence of others who act as witnesses both to the taking and the fulfillment of the vows. This phenomenon is not unique to a specific culture or creed; it can be found across the globe in religious and secular contexts. Christian vows are made to God or in the presence of God. A vow forms a relationship between the person making the vow and God, as well as with the others in the community.

But do vows work? What gives us confidence that we are going to be able to keep them, any more than the promises people make and break on a daily basis?

My wife Linda and I took membership vows in the Bruderhof church community thirty-two years ago. We had come to the Bruderhof a few years earlier, in 1987, from Minnesota. We grew up as regular American kids of the sixties. We found faith in Jesus in the late seventies and began a search to find out where God was calling us and how we might serve him and his kingdom. We wanted to find a place where we could give our all and where life was not compartmentalized but integrated – where worship, work, education, parenting, and care of the elderly were part of a life lived with others who believed what we had come to believe.

After years of searching we found the Bruderhof and made a one-week visit. Months later we returned for a longer visit, and then we came to stay. We were part of the community for a couple of years before taking our vows. This gave both us and the Bruderhof time to discern whether God was calling us to this specific community and way of life. That process will vary depending on the individual, but it is never hasty.

In the Bruderhof the act of taking vows is a sign of giving oneself completely, binding oneself unreservedly, to the service of Jesus Christ in the church community. The vows commit us to future action: to proclaim Jesus in word and deed; to give everything for the sake of Jesus, including our strength, energy, creativity, and property; to go wherever the church needs us; to do whatever task the community assigns us; to speak honestly

Randall Gauger is a pastor in the Bruderhof communities in the United States. He and his wife, Linda, live at the Fox Hill community in New York.

and accept correction; to repent and change when necessary; and to remain faithful to these vows for life.

Those promises are a very tall order if you take them seriously! When I think of them again now, I ask myself how in the world a weak, sinful, ordinary human being can hope to fulfill those all-encompassing vows. Of course, I have failed to keep my vows at times: I have bristled when people came with an admonition; I have grumbled at certain assignments I didn't feel suited to; I have held my tongue when I could have witnessed to Jesus.

BUT DO THE VOWS THEMSELVES help hold us to the path of faithfulness? I think they do. A movie scene formulated this question in my mind a new way. Ridley Scott's 2005 film *Kingdom of Heaven* tells a fictional story set in the time of the Crusades. In one scene Jerusalem is surrounded by a vast army of Muslims who intend to take back the city. In the city are mostly peasants, old men and women, children, servants, and slaves. There are no knights to defend the city except one, Balian, tasked with the defense of Jerusalem. The patriarch of Jerusalem, realizing the hopelessness of the defense, wants to flee with Balian and leave the people to the invading army, but Balian refuses to abandon the city. The patriarch tries to bring Balian to his senses by saying, "My lord, how are we to defend Jerusalem without knights? We have no knights!"

Balian responds by saying "Truly?" while gazing intently at a young boy who is a servant of the patriarch. Balian says to the boy, "You were born a servant? Kneel! Every man at arms or capable of bearing them, kneel! On your knees!" After the crowd kneels, Balian leads them in taking the vows of a knight: "Be without fear in the face of your enemies.

Bruderhof Vows of Membership

This reading is taken from the Bruderhof's community rule,
Foundations of Our Faith and Calling (Plough, 2014).

THE ACT OF TAKING VOWS is a sign of giving oneself completely and binding oneself unreservedly to the service of Christ in church community. Through this solemn and public act we pledge to no longer claim anything for ourselves, out of love to Christ. Our example is Mary the mother of Jesus, who said: "Here am I, the servant of the Lord; let it be with me according to your word."

Jesus told those who wished to follow him: "Whoever would save his life will lose it, and whoever loses his life for my sake will find it." He also taught: "When you have done all that is commanded you, say, 'We are unworthy servants; we have only done what was our duty.'"

It is in this sense that we take our vows.

Vows of membership are made in the spirit of the traditional monastic vows of poverty, chastity, and obedience:

Poverty: We pledge to give up all property and to live simply, in complete freedom from possessions.

Chastity: We pledge to uphold sexual purity and, if married, to stay faithful in the bond of marriage between one man and one woman for life.

Obedience: We pledge to yield ourselves up in obedience to Christ and our brothers and sisters, promising to serve the church

Be brave and upright that God may love thee. Speak the truth even if it should lead to your death. Safeguard the helpless. That is your oath! Rise a knight! Rise a knight!"

The Patriarch thinks Balian has lost his mind and once more tries to convince him of his folly by mockery: "Who do you think you are? Will you alter the world? Does making a man a knight make him a better fighter?" And Balian's simple answer is "Yes!"

As a pastor in my community (one of those tasks the community asked me to do) I have had many chances to meet with young people wishing to take their membership vows. I have often thought back to the scene of Balian on the walls of Jerusalem. In fact, I have shown many of them the movie clip to drive the point home: taking these vows can make them better fighters for God's kingdom. One young woman wrote back to me later:

It's been three years since I made my vows, and I've failed them hundreds of times already. But that has not changed the reality of those vows for me. They are always there for me to fall back on and reaffirm. I can't imagine where I would be had I run away from making a commitment to Jesus, but it certainly wouldn't be here in the church. I need those vows, spoken in front of the congregation, to hold me to my commitment.

Since my baptism, there have been several times when tragedy has tested my faith. I recently got to a point where I could not say with certainty that I believed anything or hoped for anything, but could merely cling to the knowledge that there was a time when I had had certainty, and try to remain faithful as best I could to what I knew I had once had, and pray for that certainty again. It's a desert stretch of

community wherever and however we are asked.

Vows of membership are made publicly, to God and before the church community, by answering the following questions:

1. Do you promise to proclaim Jesus in word and deed, for the rest of your life?

2. Are you certain that this way of brotherly and sisterly community, based on a firm faith in God and in Jesus Christ, is the way to which God has called you?

3. Are you willing, for the sake of Christ, to put yourself completely at the disposal of the church community to the end of your life – all your faculties, the entire strength of your body and soul, and all your property, both that which you now possess and that which you may later inherit or earn?

4. Will you accept admonition, when justified, and will you yourself admonish others if you sense within our community life something that should be clearer or would more fittingly express the will of God?

5. Because a living church will always be a repenting church, do you affirm and uphold the practice of church discipline, and will you be ready to ask for it yourself if necessary?

6. Are you firmly decided to remain loyal and true, bound with us in the service of love as brothers and sisters in building up church community, outreach to all people, and the proclamation of the gospel?

Upon answering yes, the new member receives the laying on of hands in the prayer that God will fill him or her anew with the Holy Spirit. ⇀

Image from Alamy. Used by permission.

life that is made all the worse for not being able to see the end of it, but my vows hold me when I wouldn't otherwise have the strength to keep going. I have found that such crises of faith ultimately strengthen my commitment by challenging it.

What this young woman describes I have also heard from others who, when going through difficult times in their lives, have returned to their vows and remembered the moment they made them. I can remind them that their brothers and sisters – who heard their vows and have made the same vows – will walk with them and support them through these difficult times.

In a recent weekday worship service here (the community gathers most evenings, outdoors when the weather allows) we were discussing commitment. One of the older brothers offered this analogy, borrowed loosely from Eugene H. Peterson's *The Unnecessary Pastor*:

> When rock climbers are climbing particularly treacherous routes, they use something called a piton, a metal spike, which they drive into the rock face and then loop their rope through to secure themselves from falling. Each time we make a vow such as in baptism or marriage, we are banging in another piton for ourselves. As we continue to climb up, we might slip a little or even fall, but that piton will be there to catch us. We might even climb down and try to find another way up, but eventually when we realize that there is no other way up and return to where we were to begin with, those pitons will still be there to hold us steady as we climb.

Vows are important, whether they are marriage vows, vows of membership, or personal vows people make to help them remember what kind of person they want to be. You see, God hears our vows and honors them. Through the Holy Spirit, he moves us to action and faithfulness. Vows are not about how good we are, how smart we are, or how strong of will we are. They are about what kind of person God wants us to be, and what we want to be. In the end, do these vows make us better fighters for God? With Balian, I firmly believe the answer is "Yes!"

Susanna Bauer, *All Around*, magnolia leaf and cotton thread, 2019

Autumn in Chrysalis-Time

It's butterfly-dying time
Leaf-grieving and thieving time
Blue wings-against-pavement time
Less praise than appraisal time

It's foxes hightailing-it time
Bird's nest-unveiling time
It's prey-caught-dangling time
In silk strands strangling time

It's wood-stoves burning up time
First frost delivering time
It's whip-poor-wills woeful in time
It's what-you-will, winging through time

It's wildfire-weathering time
Last-chance-and-gunning-it time
Lives lost believing in time
Least harm in leaving in time

It's mantises feeding off time
What's-past-releasing-us time
Cold front confronting-us time
Cicadas' arcadian time

It's rainforests blazing through time
Glaciers once greater than time
Bee colonies bleeding through time
Lost stars trespassing in time

Or is it healing time
Grave thoughts, grief leaving in time
What's sure to follow in time
Foreseen in chrysalis-time

NED BALBO

Note: Though some butterflies and moths are known to migrate or hibernate in colder weather, the adults of most species die shortly after the end of their reproductive cycle. Offspring (formerly caterpillars) may "overwinter" in a chrysalis where they develop into butterflies.

ANDREAS KNAPP

Poverty

Those who, like Francis of Assisi, reject wealth and
possessions find the whole world is theirs.

Photograph courtesy of Tim Arai

Leipzig, Germany

ultra-wealthy and the dirt-poor. How does such injustice arise?

We humans all have the same natural needs: food, clothing, shelter. Ever since humans have existed, however, we have competed for and fought over these basic things. In part, this is because in a given time and place the necessities of life may be in short supply, depending on the economic context, the climate, and so on. This results in a perceived need for a stockpiling economy, which is often as not combined with greed, and this leads to the accumulation of excessive reserves. So we appropriate more than we really need. And once the ball gets rolling, an entire economic system develops that drives people to consume more and more, and to hanker after greater and greater luxury.

Sociopsychological factors play a major role here: people are always comparing themselves with others and wanting to acquire the same things that others have. Possessions confer status, and those who want to be regarded as worth something must be able to signal their worth by means of their wealth. People also have deep anxieties: life is precarious in many ways and subject to forces such as serious illness, war, and death. And so people feel they have to protect themselves and try to secure their existence by means of collecting material possessions.

This sort of defense mechanism is a leading cause of the gaping economic differences between and within societies, and the chief reason for the exploitation of one class of people by another. Ironically, it always ends in untold misery, more often than not in armed conflict. Oddly, because the acquisition of possessions has such great significance, it is

THE WORLD IS ENTRUSTED TO US AS a gift from God. And because all people are God's children, they all have a right to the resources the world offers them. It is so rich that no one should have to go hungry or suffer want or need. But the world's goods are hardly equally distributed. On the contrary, there are atrocious disparities between the

---

Andreas Knapp is a member of the Little Brothers of the Gospel in Leipzig, Germany. He is the author of The Last Christians: Stories of Persecution, Flight, and Resilience in the Middle East *(Plough, 2017).*

Photograph courtesy of Quinn Norton

Warsaw, Poland

frequently interpreted in religious terms: the wealthy must be blessed by God. Wealth itself thus assumes a divine dimension. In the end, we find ourselves worshipping and revering the god Mammon: the golden calf, symbol of idolatrous materialism.

1. The Prophetic Critique of Wealth

According to the Bible, this world is a creation, a gift of God for all people. But greed and envy have largely destroyed the paradise-like home God intended and intends for them.

Humans have become like wolves toward their fellow beings. And because no one thinks they are getting enough, it leads, generation after generation, to oppression, theft, and war.

The prophets of the Old Testament repeatedly denounce the idolization of material goods that leads to this. First and foremost, they chastise the powerful for enslaving the poor and depriving them of their rights: "Listen, you heads of Jacob and rulers of the house of Israel! Should you not know justice? – you who hate the good and love the evil" (Mic. 3:1–2).

For these prophets, the equitable behavior that stems from solidarity with the weak and disadvantaged becomes the touchstone of true worship: "I hate, I despise your festivals, and I take no delight in your solemn assemblies. . . . I will not listen to the melody of your harps. But let justice roll down like water and righteousness like an ever-flowing stream" (Amos 5:21–24). In this way, the prophets proclaim a God who sides with the poor and the exploited.

Jesus of Nazareth places himself completely in line with this thinking. Because his life is rooted in devotion to God, he has no need of wealth – no need to be somebody. He is content to be the "beloved Son of God." In fact, he distances himself from all material possessions. And since he sees love of God as the deepest fulfillment, he has no need for anxious or petty calculations. He freely gives of his time, his energy, his whole life. By means of his generous spirit, he makes visible the generosity of God, who lets his sun rise over both the good and the evil (Matt. 5:45).

Jesus has special affection for the outsiders, the sick, and the poor. Meanwhile he warns the well-off again and again about the dangers of their wealth: "But woe to you who are rich, for you have received your consolation" (Luke 6:24). Those who desire to follow Jesus must dispense with the external safeguards provided by property. They must put all their trust in God, who will in turn provide them with all they need. And their hearts cannot remain tied to outer things; God alone must be their treasure.

Those who enter this school of life gain the freedom that allows them to let go of possessions. Whoever looks to God and imitates Christ's selflessness and largesse escapes the trap of measuring himself against others and turning into a rival. Those who accept and embody Jesus' self-forgetful friendship will turn to their neighbors uninhibitedly and assist in building a culture of true humanity and justice.

2. Poverty and the Early Church

In confessing Jesus as the Christ, the Son of God, the first Christians opened their eyes to God's preference for the lowly. In Jesus, God chose not only a human destiny, but more than that: he chose to be a little man from a despised village. "Can anything good come out of Nazareth?" (John 1:46). God was not born to parents of noble lineage or to the priestly class, but into a simple family who worked with their hands. In this way, God's option for the poor comes to expression. Human hierarchies, built as they are around money and power, are hereby upended. Precisely those who do not count for much according to human standards are invited to experience their dignity as children of God.

The apostle Paul repeatedly marvels over the descent of Christ, "who, though he existed in the form of God, did not regard equality with God as something to be grasped, but emptied himself, taking the form of a slave" (Phil. 2:6–7). "For you know the generous act of our Lord Jesus Christ, that though he was rich, yet for your sakes he became poor, so that by his poverty you might become rich." (2 Cor. 8:9). If this is how God has bestowed his riches upon us – through giving us Christ's poverty – then all the riches of this world count for nothing. Worldly goods and honors are as good as rubbish (Phil. 3:8). Further, the way of Christ challenges us to work for the poor and weak and to build a more just society.

It was out of this conviction that the first Christian communities opted for a new way of living – one that functioned without private property. "All who believed were together and had all things in common; they would sell their possessions and goods and distribute

Owners and Heirs

Ernesto Cardenal

At first glance, we all own nature, from the earth with all its landscapes to the starry skies. Yet as soon as we claim ownership of even a few acres of land, none of it belongs to us any longer. Only when we are poor can we call the whole world our own, as the birds call the sky their own, and as Francis of Assisi called all earthly things his. This is why he spoke of poverty as a great treasure, and why he said that it is a great luxury to eat at a beautiful boulder next to a refreshing spring under a blue sky, while the rich (who are really poor) are confined to dining rooms with four walls and limited dimensions.

God is the Lord of the entire world, and as God's children we are heirs to its riches. Surrounded by immeasurable wealth, we need only reach out to take hold of it all. A handful of water, even if it runs between our fingers, is no less valuable than a handful of diamonds.

And yet, again – as soon as someone purchases a piece of land and fences it in, he relinquishes his right to all the rest. . . .

It follows that Christian poverty does not imply owning just a little, but owning *nothing at all*, so as to be able to call everything one's own. The monk does not limit his possessions to a few things; rather, he gives up all, and thus owns all: air, sun, earth, sky, and sea. Without greed, detached from everything, we too may possess everything.

Ernesto Cardenal, *Vida en el amor* (Carlos Lohlé, 1970).

the proceeds to all, as any had need" (Acts 2:44–45). They saw that it is not possessions that count, but familial care and communion.

This is also how the earliest monastic communities arose. According to tradition, Saint Anthony the Great (d. 356), the son of wealthy parents in Lower Egypt, was deeply affected by this specific word from the Gospel of Matthew: "If you wish to be perfect, go, sell your possessions, and give the money to the poor, and you will have treasure in heaven; then come, follow me" (19:21). After giving away his possessions, Anthony retreated to a life of solitude and frugality. He was soon joined by disciples, and the monastic way of life that grew up around them eventually drew men and women from across Egypt, Palestine, and Syria. This great movement admittedly had several points of origin: on the one hand, the famous desert fathers and mothers who attracted so many by their example; on the other, it was a phenomenon whose reforms point directly to the gospel, in opposition to a church that had meanwhile become wealthy and powerful.

3. Again and Again, the Call to Poverty

Even as the early church developed a hierarchy, its call to poverty did not fall silent. John Chrysostom, patriarch in the imperial city of Constantinople, was tireless in preaching against pomp and luxury; moreover, he acted as a spokesman for the poor and appealed to the consciences of the well-heeled and the influential. To him, community of goods, as cultivated among the first Christians, was the ideal way to address property. Like other fathers of the church, he criticized the institution of private property, which entails the accumulation of things by one person who holds on to more than he needs, at the expense of another, who suffers deprivation: "How is it conceivable for a wealthy person to be a good

one?" he asked. "It is impossible. He can only attain goodness to the degree that he shares his wealth with others." According to Chrysostom, a truly rich person is one who gives away his possessions to the poor.

In the High Middle Ages, when the church was at a pinnacle of power and wealth, gospel-based movements arose whose adherents cultivated voluntary poverty. Perhaps the most famous of these was the one that sprang up around Francis of Assisi (1181/82–1226). Through his own experience, Francis had been enlightened by the painful recognition that, like a drug, money has the capacity to addict and destroy a soul. Not long after this, he bequeathed his inheritance to a church – and was promptly taken to court by his father, a wealthy merchant.

Striking out on his own, Francis consistently warned against wealth and, in particular, the idolizing of material things and the tendency to cling to one's money. Possessions, he argued, can end up possessing their owner. He refused to touch money – for example, coins he found on the street. Like Jesus, he preached the sort of poverty that sets the soul free. In doing so, he did not romanticize the hardships that so often afflict people, sometimes driving them to despair. Nor did the simple life he advocated have anything to do with a compulsive abnegation. Rather, he espoused a voluntary, almost playful poverty that engendered liberation from things, and consequently opened new spaces and new relationships. And he and his followers discovered how this freedom results in fraternity, allowing

London, United Kingdom

people to see their fellow human beings as brothers and sisters, and moving them to share with one another.

Again, Francis of Assisi did not embrace the simple life in order to promote self-denial as an end in itself. But he did consciously choose poverty because of the meaning he had discovered in it, which he discerned to be in keeping with the gospel. It was, as he saw it, a way of assimilating his own practice with the teachings of Jesus and, at the same time, a way of demonstrating solidarity with the involuntarily poor.

> **Because no human is self-created, we ought to approach life as a gift from God, one that cannot to be measured in mere possessions to which an individual might be tempted to lay claim.**

At the same time, his frugal manner of living gave him a new latitude in finding communion with like-minded people. In other words, far from being grim, his lifestyle breathed something joyous, cheerful, and light. Lady Poverty became Francis's great love, the bride to whom he was betrothed. And those who joined him were expected to share this love, and also had to renounce all of their possessions. Even mundane items such as clothes were regarded as being held in trust, rather than owned. Through this radical orientation to the gospel, numerous communities arose after the example of Francis, striving to lead a more fraternal and just way of life, both in spirit and practice.

4. The Vow of Poverty and the Gift Economy

In the context of early Christian monasticism, the religious vow of poverty is not primarily an act of renunciation but implies living together with others, as a natural consequence of brotherhood or sisterhood. This is because in a truly communal life the social roles normally associated with property do not apply. There are no nobles, commoners, or slaves, but all are "brothers" and "sisters" – a designation that reflects the nurturing of a family-like structure characterized by mutual love and responsibility. In this way, a vow of poverty obviates competitive attitudes with regard to material things.

Notably, this vow is not intended to elevate misery, nor is the point to dispense with material things. Material goods are not despised per se. Rather, the vow reflects a basic attitude: because no human is self-created, we ought to approach life as a gift from God, one that cannot to be measured in mere possessions to which an individual might be tempted to lay claim.

In his book *The Gift,* Lewis Hyde identifies two economies. In a "needs economy," material goods are viewed in terms of who owns them, and economic activity is naturally directed toward acquisition. The goal is to remove as many economic goods as possible from general circulation and to acquire them as private holdings. Since material goods are limited, it follows that the person who has more things will have more prestige and power.

One consequence of such a system is that individuals always want more than they actually need. Before long, they will not only amass possessions for real needs, but for potential ones as well, and end up hoarding wealth that cannot really be used but only flaunted. The hallmarks of such an economy are greed, jealousy, the accumulation of goods (and with it, social prestige), and, finally, readiness for conflict, if necessary, in order to defend one's property and possessions.

What Hyde calls the "gift economy" is marked by a completely different set of characteristics. Here, material goods are seen first and foremost as resources entrusted to the user by God, by nature, and by the community. And as gifts, they are also to be passed on to others. In a "gift economy," economic activity consists primarily in maintaining the free flow of goods, contributing to the well-being of the greater community by means of one's own labor and talents, and fairly distributing material things. Possessions are measured in terms of actual (not merely perceived) needs, and no one privately owns the resources that everyone depends on – for example, land, water, and food. The virtues that guide such a system include generosity, simplicity, community, and compassion. Displays of wealth are seen as vulgar expressions of unnecessary consumption.

In a religious community, a rule of poverty ought to be a concretization of such a gift economy. At its root stands faith in God, the author and giver of all gifts, and the recognition that we humans are not to appropriate them for private use, but rather ought to ensure that they are kept accessible to all, so that they might benefit all.

The renunciation of private property in religious life should be a prophetic sign to a world in which property is idolized. Voluntary poverty is a visible form of protest against the dictatorship of acquiring and possessing. Simultaneously, it implies solidarity with those whose penury is not voluntary but enforced. This solidarity is made visible when those who have taken a religious vow of poverty place themselves at the side of the involuntarily poor in order to strive together for a more just world.

I lived in Bolivia for several years and got to know a priest who was also a trained gardener and taught many people how to grow vegetables. I wanted to plant an herb bed in our community garden and asked this priest

From the Rule of Life of the Little Brothers of the Gospel

Christ gives us a treasure that fills our hearts. He impels us to leave everything and become poor in spiritual as well as material things.

We embrace poverty with our whole heart. Wealth is not only an unwieldy burden, but a danger. In fact, it is not compatible with love of neighbor, because whatever you keep for yourself you cannot share with others.

We want to become poor in spirit and free from every possessive desire, whether for money or material goods. Further, we want to share the working conditions of the poor. This will help us make their longings and just demands our own.

Constitutions des Petits Frères de l'Evangile, Bruxelles 1985.

for some seedlings. I was more than a little surprised when he arrived at my door one day with a whole load of sand and gravel in addition to the plants. When I inquired, he explained: "You have excellent soil, but herbs develop their aroma best in lean soil. You will want to mix the sand and gravel into the soil." He then added, "It's just like the spiritual life. In fat times – when there is too much, when things are going too well – a religious community will not develop as it should, let alone thrive. But in poor, lean soil it will flourish." ⤳

This article was translated from German by Chris Zimmerman.

SR. CARINO HODDER, OP

DEMYSTIFYING

Chastity

It's time to rediscover chastity as
a virtue for everyone.

MY DECISION TO JOIN A CONVENT was one of the best things that ever happened to my dating life. At the time I found this unusual – and frankly alarming – but I have since come to learn that this phenomenon is, while not exactly normal, certainly not unheard of. After all, human beings are hardwired by nature to seek the good, and so any person who earnestly and openly seeks the supernatural good of a life of celibate chastity is going to find her natural desire for the good of marriage deepened and purified at the same time. This process is logical and organic, and explains why I spent the year before entering religious life accepting several unexpected but not entirely unwelcome invitations to dinner from pleasant single young men, wondering if this

N. C. Wyeth, *Herons in Summer,* oil on canvas, 1941

Sister Carino Hodder, OP, is a Dominican Sister of St Joseph based in Hampshire, England. She made her First Profession in September 2019.

was really a prudent use of my time when sitting on my desk back home was an application form for the convent filled out and ready to be posted.

This experience of romantic entanglement during my aspirancy, oscillating between praying for the grace to persevere in the religious calling I was about to embark upon and wondering what my first name would sound like coupled with one boy or another's surname, was a highly practical schooling in the true nature of celibate chastity. It showed me very clearly, though not without a good deal of emotional chaos, that entering a religious order was not intended to be a flight from my natural human desire for love and intimacy. As I passed from aspirancy to postulancy, from novitiate to temporary profession, that first lesson in celibate chastity held fast: I found the religious life does not – and, indeed, should not – decouple a person from her sexuality, as if it were a cumbersome bolt-on to human nature that could only hinder and obstruct the path to holiness. Instead, religious life is the means by which God perfects and fulfills every aspect of our human nature, sexuality included, through union with the One who gave that nature to us in the first place.

SPEAKING FROM MY OWN WESTERN Catholic tradition, I refer to *celibate* chastity when talking of the evangelical counsel of chastity by which I live. This is because there

is nothing about chastity per se that makes it the sole preserve of consecrated religious. Chastity, according to the catechism of the Catholic Church, is simply "the successful integration of sexuality within the person." It is the process by which "sexuality, in which man's belonging to the bodily and biological world is expressed," is made "personal and truly human" through appropriate and rightly-ordered relationships. There is nothing in this definition about renouncing marriage and sexual relations. The call to chastity applies just as much to spouses and to single people looking for romance as it does to consecrated religious, for all the faithful are called to a graced integration of our sexuality with our desires and our state of life. To put a more Thomistic spin on it, chastity is the virtue by which the natural inclination toward relation-ship is perfected; and thus anybody who possesses such an inclination – that's all of us, to be clear – is called to have it perfected by the integrating and ordering means of chastity. Chastity is for all the faithful, whether we are married or single, and whether our singleness is permanent and willed or merely temporary.

For many people, the virtue of chastity will be made manifest in the way they pursue their romantic relations and, if these result in marriage, how they live out their married life. For those still searching for a spouse, the prac-tice of chastity will enliven and redeem this period of looking, transforming it from simply an anteroom to marriage into a school of virtue and a fruitful time of intimacy with the Lord.

For a small minority, however, chastity will be manifest in a life of celibacy, in which marriage and family life are, by the grace of God, freely and permanently renounced. But why? Why does a life of radical consecration to God necessarily involve the renunciation of something so good and so fundamental to our nature? Various quick, easy, and deeply misleading answers spring to mind: to give more time for ministry; because sexual appetites are a distraction from a life of prayer and spirituality; because, let's be honest, these people wouldn't have made good spouses and parents anyway.

None of these answers are adequate, ultimately because none of them make reference to the source and archetype of religious life: Christ himself. Jesus, "the chaste, poor, and obedient one," as Pope Saint John Paul II puts it in *Vita consecrata*, calls us to this life in order that we might be conformed to him. Did Jesus ever counsel removing oneself from other people's needs and concerns in order to make more time for work? Does Jesus, accused of being a glutton and a drunkard – who, as the Holy Father Pope Francis describes him in *Laudato si'*, "was far removed from philosophies which despised the body, matter, and the things of the world" – counsel a fearful spurning of the flesh for spiritual health? Does Jesus, who blesses little children (Mark 10:16) and loves his disciples with the love of the Father (John 15:9), eschew the love of family life because he would have been bad at it?

He does none of these things. At no point in his public ministry does Jesus preach against the good of marriage; quite the opposite, in fact. In Matthew 19, as part of his teaching on divorce, Jesus asks his interlocutors, "Have you not read that the one who made them at the beginning *made them male and female*, and said, *For this reason a man shall leave his father and mother and be joined to his wife, and the two shall become one flesh*?" Yet in the same chapter of Matthew, Jesus introduces a teaching that is distinct and unprecedented: the teaching that it is possible, in fact praiseworthy, to renounce marriage for the sake of God. "For there are eunuchs who have been so from birth, and there are eunuchs who have been made eunuchs by others, and there are eunuchs who have made themselves eunuchs for the sake of the kingdom of heaven. Let anyone accept this who can." This was a highly unusual position to take in the context of the Hebrew tradition.

But what is clear from the gospel is that, in the eyes of the incarnate Lord, celibate

> The call to chastity applies just as much to spouses and to single people looking for romance as it does to consecrated religious.

chastity is not simply a privation of marriage and sexual intimacy. Instead, it is a positive choice for good. It is celibacy *for the sake of the kingdom of heaven* that Christ counsels, not celibacy as the mere absence of marriage. In other words, a person's celibacy has to be *for* something – something greater than herself, something greater even than marriage – in order to be fruitful. Truly chaste and authentic celibacy must recognize that, ultimately, it is not working against marriage and family life, but instead is ordered toward the same goal: eternal life in the kingdom of heaven. One of the purposes of celibate chastity is to serve as a reminder – a sign, in fact – that, for all its joys and blessings, the married life is only a means to an end; as Christ tells us, we shall neither marry nor be given in marriage at the resurrection (Matt. 22:30).

Celibate chastity, then, is both eschatological and prophetic: it not only points forward to the final state of all sanctified human beings in the kingdom of God, but also demonstrates how that kingdom is already present among us here today through the church. It is the means by which the Lord focuses our whole selves, as one chaste and integrated whole, *on* him and *for* him, to show forth to the church the life we shall all live in the beatific vision. As Saint Cyprian told the consecrated virgins of the early church, "You have begun to be what we shall be." Indeed, the history of the church is replete with these prophetic signs of our

My grief at not having children would not be healed by approaching celibacy as a lifelong endurance test.

eschatological future, men and women whose example of graced chastity is presented to us anew each year in the unfolding of the liturgy: saints such as Agnes, Agatha, and Lucy from the early centuries, up to Josephine Bakhita and Maria Goretti from our modern era.

These are wonderful examples of the blessings of the life of celibate chastity, but for me what is most striking about their lives is how dramatically and disturbingly eventful they often were. In many cases, eschewing marriage and sexual relations set these women radically at odds with non-Christian society's expectations of them and even put them in conflict with their own families. It is unsurprising that the terms used to describe virginity and martyrdom are elided in the liturgy: both are spoken of as crowns of victory, won at great cost and manifesting all-consuming love. These women's choice for Christ alone, to the exclusion of any earthly romantic attachment, so often sent shockwaves through their communities, and to this day can strike us as baffling and wasteful. This is another connection between chastity and martyrdom: both are the kind of total commitment, an utter

gift of one's whole self, that can only be made sense of if it is viewed entirely separately from our human desires for comfort, convenience, or good standing with others. It is only in the light of God's grace that these callings can be understood – whether by the casual observer or the person living it.

HERE IS MY OWN EXPERIENCE. WHEN I began work as a parish sister for a church in North London last year, I found myself receiving more insight into family life than I had ever had before. Every week I met children who wanted to snuggle against me as we read the Bible together, hold my hand as we walked from the hall to the church, or be comforted by me when they injured themselves playing; every week I met parents who talked of their spouses and their children with such joy and affection, such pride, that I felt I could sit and listen and ask questions for hours. But over time I began to sense something unhealthy, almost obsessive, in my approach to this ministry. When I exposed these misgivings in prayer, the divine Physician gave me an unexpected diagnosis: I was becoming obsessed with ministering to these families because I wanted a family myself, and I was trying to process the fact that I would never have one.

When I entered religious life in my early twenties I had no particular attraction to the idea of starting a family. I certainly wanted to get married, but my desire for marriage was founded on a vision of marital life as a lifelong adventure shared by two adults, and I was indifferent to whether or not children might be added to the mix. To discover a deep longing for children only after I had committed never to have any was profoundly hurtful in a way that is difficult to put into words and, I sense, not intended to be. All I can say is that the grief I experienced was leavened with such interior peace and such confidence in the gentleness of

God's guiding hand that I could not but trust that this realization of mine had taken place at the time the Lord appointed for it.

It was the counsel of a priest that helped me to realize this. A Dominican friar based in the United States delivered a series of lectures on Saint Thomas Aquinas's teaching on virginity to my sisters over Zoom in the academic term I began work as a parish sister. He concluded one of these lectures by saying that the key to living celibate chastity fruitfully is to see it not as a burden or as an imposition, but as a gift that God makes to his beloved, so that he or she may live completely for him. An understanding of celibate chastity that is primarily functional or utilitarian – more time for ministry, fewer attachments to be uprooted from when moving between convents, and so on – cannot and will not sustain a person over the course of her religious life. My grief would not be healed by burying my desire for children and approaching celibacy as a lifelong endurance test. It would be healed by accepting celibacy as God's means of working in me to bring me to himself; of choosing to rejoice, rather than to lament, that I am my beloved's and my beloved is mine.

Consecrated life is not for disembodied spirits, but for human beings. The sisters in my convent come from a wide variety of backgrounds, with vast and often baffling differences in personality, temperament, and sense of humor, but here is the one thing we have in common: we were created as human beings, we were redeemed as human beings, we are being saved as human beings, and for all eternity, whether in our current earthly sojourn or in the joy of the beatific vision, we will *live* as human beings. We are each a union of body and soul. We each have physical desires and attractions; we each need fellowship and intimacy; we each long to care and be cared for. It is this human nature, in all its fragility and wonder, that each one of us has brought before Christ in religious consecration so that he might bind it to himself. It is for the perfection of this human nature that he counsels us to live as chaste, impoverished, and obedient disciples of him.

This article is very much a dispatch from the trenches. I entered religious life as a postulant five years ago, first professed my obedience to the Rule by which I live two years ago, and will renew it permanently in Final Profession this September. I hardly need to point out that five years is absolutely nothing in the grand scheme of things, especially since the evangelical counsels are, for the most part, slow burners: I dare say there's a providential reason why most religious don't go out in a blaze of sanctity after eight years in the style of Thérèse of Lisieux. We live within time, and it takes time to integrate, to heal, and to grow in the way that the evangelical counsel of chastity makes possible. There are new depths to my relationship with the Lord, new vistas of understanding of what it means to have been given the gift of celibacy, that I am still discovering.

My life of celibate chastity is only just beginning, and all I can really say for certain is that the peace and the joy that comes from a life of chaste consecration is entirely beyond my understanding or my merit. This life is a gift of which I am wholly unworthy, and the closest I can come to giving adequate thanks is simply to live it as best I can.

NORANN VOLL

THE ADVENTURE OF
Obedience

It's not popular. But obedience can transplant us
to places we never expected.

When humans have become as perfect in voluntary obedience as the inanimate creation is in its lifeless obedience, then they will put on its glory, or rather that greater glory of which Nature is only the first sketch.
—C. S. Lewis

THE GREEK MEANING OF THE WORD obedience is to "listen under." Twenty years ago, my husband, Chris, and I left New York and arrived Down Under on the back of the Millennial Drought. A vow of obedience got us here. After the longest journey of our lives, we emerged exhausted into the arrivals hall at Sydney airport, our two-year-old and ten-week-old sons clinging to us like little koalas. Knowingly, Chris looked at me, dug in my handbag and, holding out my hairbrush, said, "I've got the kids." When I returned newly brushed, a glass of white wine sweated

Photographs by Norann Voll

Norann Voll lives at the Danthonia Bruderhof in rural Australia with her husband, Chris. They have three sons. She writes about discipleship, motherhood, and feeding people.

by a bowl of Thai noodle soup. My first sip of crisp Australian chardonnay ("chardy," as I'd soon learn to call it) conjured up tears. My man knew just what I needed. But the day did not finish there.

We boarded smaller and smaller planes, flying over scorched earth, empty farm ponds ("dams"), and thin cattle. As the local mail plane landed in Inverell, apparently the "Sapphire City," kangaroos bounded over brick-red dirt alongside the runway. We were

The seasons were backwards, the food different. I didn't know anyone. My life looked like the inside of my refrigerator: I hardly recognized a single thing.

four and a half years into our marriage. *Five years is the sapphire anniversary,* I thought. *Please let us be rid of this place by then.*

An hour later, we arrived, welcomed by our Bruderhof church-community, forty other brothers and sisters, most of whom were imports like us. They had been braving this land for a couple of years already, and had set about the task of converting our new home, "Danthonia," from a single-family sheep farm to a place of welcome for many. Chris and I and our boys were ushered to our new apartment, in the original homestead. The freshly cleaned wool carpets gave off a gentle lanolin odor. We collapsed gratefully into bed, waking the next morning to the scent of jacaranda and the song of magpies, and butterflies tapping a tattoo on our window.

This place has a wonderful ruggedness to it that I love, I wrote to my parents a week or so later. *Over our house blooms a purple jacaranda tree, and around it are pink and white oleander bushes. There are wild storms and calm dawns; it's a country whose impetuousness repeatedly catches me off guard.* But my attempts to embrace the newness quickly wore off, and my journal became a place of refuge for my feelings of lostness: *I feel horrendously lonely and dry inside. Every night we watch the bushfires in the range of hills south of us. I know we're safe – the fires aren't as close as they appear at night – but still I hold my little bub tight as I look out at the eerie glow.*

The seasons were backwards, the food different. I didn't know anyone. My life looked like the inside of my refrigerator: I hardly recognized a single thing. *What am I doing here?* I found myself sitting with this question again and again, even as my heart already whispered the answer.

I WAS TWENTY YEARS OLD WHEN I KNEW God was calling me – giving me a vocation – to join the Bruderhof, an intentional Christian community that shares all things in common and seeks to live in total devotion to Jesus and his kingdom. All full members of the Bruderhof take lifelong vows. I remember the moment when I shared my decision with my father. He told me I had just signed up for the biggest adventure of my life. After several years of testing my calling – and gaining a deeper

understanding through firsthand experience of faith-based community comprised of "warts and all" people – I took my vows.

The vows are unequivocal (see page 52). You place yourself "completely at the disposal of the church community to the end of your life – all your faculties, the entire strength of your body and soul, and all your property, both that which you now possess and that which you may later inherit or earn." But it is the joyous and unique wording of the last question I answered that day that I've found myself returning to most often in the years since: "Are you firmly decided to remain loyal and true, bound with us in the service of love as brothers and sisters in building up church community, outreach to all people, and the proclamation of the gospel?" I love the phrase "bound with us in the service of love" because it remains a daily call to action, an invitation to this radical way of living and striving for discipleship alongside others. Obedience to this vow is no dry and dutiful affair.

Unsurprisingly, my dad reminded me of the adventure conversation some years later when Chris and I told him that we were engaged (both sets of parents having blessed our courtship). After all, it isn't hard to grasp that vows of obedience, whether to one's calling or to one's spouse, mean traversing the inevitable valleys and mountains of the heart, with an occasional epic pilgrimage of faith thrown in for good measure. But at the time it didn't occur to me that obedience to those vows might see me physically uprooted from all that

It is up to me to decide the quality of my vowed obedience, just as it's up to me to decide the degree to which I pursue love and joy and gentleness within my marriage.

was safe and familiar to me, sent spinning off to a new hemisphere, into new circumstances and attitudes.

But that is what happened: Chris and I were asked by our church to relocate to Australia to work alongside our brothers and sisters to build up a life of fellowship, half a world away from those we held dear. Naturally, we said yes; after all, in a mirror-version of the Benedictine vow of stability, our vows include the promise to go anywhere our church needs us, and to give it our best upon arrival. And so we went, facing our first sweltering Christmas season (believe me, "In the Bleak Midwinter" doesn't pack the same emotional impact when you're singing it with sweat trickling from your armpits while black flies swarm around your nose and eyes), looking into the night sky only to find familiar constellations upside down.

It took us a little while to find our groove – no shame in admitting that – but once we did, the beauty of our new homeland and, more importantly, the boundless possibilities for creative work all around us, opened our hearts; we began to fall in love with Australia and her people, to put down roots, to grow. However,

for me the real shift came nearly five years into our Australian adventure: I discovered I was pregnant with our long-awaited third child. Nothing went to plan. I spent most of the sweltering Australian summer months of January and February inside of hospitals with stern doctors telling me to be still or lose my child. Being physically inactive forced me into an uninvited time of quiet: I needed to remain obedient to a season of stillness to keep my child alive. This tiny being was actively growing, striving for strength, but only if held within a circle of peaceful rest.

I am a born doer; that's my love language. But for once, and for the sake of someone else, I had to stop and listen. Being still gave me a chance to consider the nature of obedience. I came to understand that just as my obedience to my body would give life to a child, obedience to my vows was not blind or claustrophobic, but a life-giving liberation to true freedom. Obedience gives rise to gifts we could never foresee, a creative transformation that begins the actual work, a setting free to receive the gifts that God has in mind for us. I was beginning to do the heart-work, the training, the learning to say yes to the small, seemingly insignificant things that allow for greater surrender.

Obedience is sometimes cast as a negative, restrictive word, but in my experience it is deeply liberating and renewing. It is up to me to decide the quality of my vowed obedience, just as it's up to me to decide the degree to which I pursue love and joy and gentleness within my marriage. With my vow of loyalty to my husband, Chris, I promise to continue that pursuit. With a vow of obedience to a church body, I promise to pursue God's truth and life and calling above all else. If obedience truly means to "listen under," I need to believe that my brothers and sisters, who form the

church to whom I've pledged my obedience, sometimes know me better than I know myself. It follows, too, that God knows my heart more deeply and my path more clearly than I could ever imagine. It is the same for each of us. Obedience should not blind and restrict, but set us on a continuous journey pursuing the heart of Jesus and his mission, with no regard for personal glory.

During my private season of patient stillness and inner growth, Australia's next drought arrived, bringing heartache to many families who rely on the land for their livelihood. This drought led our community to understand that our interactions with our land were not harmonious or sustainable. We would watch our pastureland struggle to recover between the dry seasons, and then, when the rains arrived, stare in horror as torrents washed topsoil away. So, at the beginning of the 2007 drought, we began planting trees. We took our first tentative steps toward embracing regenerative agriculture and landscape restoration. We could not have known then (as, no doubt, we do not fully recognize now) just how much work would be required, and how many false starts and missteps we'd make along the way. But we sensed something important was being set in motion: a communal obedience to the withering landscape around us, a commitment to restoration of the land – our piece of the creation God had made and deemed "good" – in the faith that healing would begin.

As we planted trees in the phosphate-crusted soil, we set life-giving stalks in barren places. We willed them to take root, to thrive, to regenerate. And slowly, they did. Our youngest was born on a day of heavenly rain, and this child's arrival was the beginning of the healing of our hearts, a new and permanent connection to this country – not the land of our birth, maybe, but perhaps of our rebirth. It was a rebirth of sorts, a realization of the miracle of obedience that had brought us here and was changing us in the best of ways. Obedience is the discovery of joy in the adventure, a joy that doesn't depend on circumstance but relishes the journey.

It takes faith to remain connected to the land, just as it takes faith to remain connected to a specific body of believers. All kinds of obstacles will crop up unexpectedly – storms, droughts, fires, floods. And yet if the obedience is there – the constancy, the commitment – order will be restored through difficulties. Obedience holds us firm when we are weakened by the elements. Obedience conducts us through hard times into fruitful seasons of regeneration; it allows us to be transplanted to places we could never have imagined ourselves thriving, and blossom in ways we never thought we could. If we don't nurture faithfulness, we never reap the fruits of obedience.

The weeks after our son's birth were like an epiphany. As wattle blossom washed our countryside in gold, and the pear, apple, and peach trees that a young war bride had planted around our homestead decades ago burst into bloom, I carried our baby out into the land I had so long struggled to love. "This is the land of your birth," I whispered, as I held him in the sun-warmth under the bee-buzzing trees, "your birthplace and my heartland." I was finally beginning to understand Mother Teresa's advice that "obedience well-lived frees us from selfishness and pride, and so it helps us to find God and in him the whole world. Obedience is a special grace, and it produces unfailing peace, inward joy, and close union with God." The new trees we planted began holding on, the healing soil began to hold the water, and when our youngest turned two, the rains returned – and stayed in abundance for the next two years. Finally, obedience bore fruit.

I cannot claim to fully understand obedience, even as I continue to live in pursuit of a life that forms a surrendered whole. Beginning to learn obedience meant tapping into a transforming power, a living surrender that began to sustain me, even as our land was beginning to reciprocate our dedication to the healing of its depletion. Obedience meant embracing stillness, creating the quiet and detachment in which "listening under" becomes possible. I have learned that obedience is the bridle that guides, the keel that steadies, the wing that lifts, the sure map that shows the trusted way.

Fishing boat,
Khirbet Beit Lei,
Israel

Vows of Baptism

*Ancient church sources from Armenia,
North Africa, England, and Moravia.*

Armenia, fourth century

The Armenian Apostolic Church is one of the most ancient Christian denominations. This Eucharistic liturgy invites the congregation to remember that their baptism washed them of sin and calls them to live in the power of the Holy Spirit and wash the world with their holy lives.

Holy Father, who has called us by the name of Thine Only Begotten, and hast enlightened us through the baptism of the spiritual font, deign to accept this holy mystery for the forgiveness of our sins; stamp upon us the graces of the Holy Ghost, as Thou didst on the holy apostles who taste of it, and became the cleansers of the whole world. . . . Look not upon the unworthiness of my sins; neither withhold from me the grace of Thy Holy Spirit. But according to Thine unspeakable charity, grant that this be for the expiation of sins, and for the loosing of trespasses.

Charles Edward Hammond, ed., *Liturgies, Eastern and Western* (Wotton-under-Edge: Clarendon Press, 1878), 163.

Deer drinking from the fountain of life, Carthage, Tunisia

North Africa, third century

Writing just over a century after the life of Christ, Tertullian reflects on the joys of those who have prepared for and finally receive the sacrament of baptism.

They who are about to enter baptism ought to pray with repeated prayers, fasts, and bendings of the knee, and vigils all the night through, and with the confession of all bygone sins, that they may express the meaning even of the baptism of John: *"They were baptized,"* says [the Scripture], *"confessing their own sins."* To us it is matter for thankfulness if we do *now* publicly confess our iniquities or our turpitudes: for we do at the same time both make satisfaction for our former sins, by mortification of our flesh and spirit, and lay beforehand the foundation of defenses against the temptations which will closely follow. . . . Therefore, blessed ones, whom the grace of God awaits, when you ascend from that most sacred font of your new birth, and spread your hands for the first time in the house of your mother, together with your brethren, ask from the Father, ask from the Lord, that His own specialties of grace and distributions of gifts [1 Cor. 12:4–12] may be supplied you. *"Ask,"* says He, *"and you shall receive."* Well, you have asked, and have received; you have knocked, and it has been opened to you. Only, I pray that, when you are asking, you be mindful likewise of Tertullian the sinner.

Alexander Roberts, James Donaldson, and A. Cleveland Coxe, eds., *Ante-Nicene Fathers* (Christian Literature Publishing Co., 1885). Revised and edited for *New Advent* by Kevin Knight.

Loaves and fishes,
Tabgha, Israel

England, sixteenth century

A central element of Anglican worship for the past five centuries, The Book of Common Prayer *was compiled by Thomas Cranmer (1489–1556) in the vernacular so that all laypeople could worship in English rather than Latin. It includes the following rite of baptism.*

Question: Dost thou renounce the devil and all his works, the vain pomp and glory of the world, with all covetous desires of the same, and the carnal desires of the flesh; so that thou wilt not follow nor be led by them?

Answer: I renounce them all.

Question: Dost thou believe in God the Father Almighty, Maker of heaven and earth?

And in Jesus Christ his only begotten Son our Lord? And that he was conceived by the Holy Ghost, born of the Virgin Mary; that he suffered under Pontius Pilate, was crucified, dead, and buried; that he went down into hell, and also did rise again the third day; that he ascended into heaven, and sitteth at the right hand of God the Father Almighty; and from thence shall come again at the end of the World, to judge the quick and the dead? And dost thou believe in the Ghost; the holy Catholick Church; the Communion of Saints; the Remission of sins; the Resurrection of the flesh; and the everlasting Life after death?

Answer: All this I stedfastly believe.

Question: Wilt thou be baptized in this faith?

Answer: That is my desire.

Question: Wilt thou then obediently keep God's holy will and commandments, and walk in the same all the days of thy life?

Answer: I will endeavour to do, God being my helper.

The Book of Common Prayer, 1662 edition as printed by John Baskerville in Cambridge in 1762.

Basket with
grapes, Maon
Synagogue,
Negev Desert

Moravia, sixteenth century

*The Anabaptists of the Reformation era
practiced rebaptism of believers who had been
baptized as infants, at a time when this was
a capital offense. This Hutterite baptismal
instruction encourages candidates to "count the
cost." Baptism should be embraced not out of
compulsion but as a free act of the will, "to the
joy and delight of your soul."*

1. The church of Christ is the gathering of the
believing and devout, the people of God who
have given up the sinful life. We are led into this
gathering by true submission. It is the spiritual
ark of Noah in which we can be preserved.

2. It is no human institution but a work of God.
Just as Mary conceived Christ through faith and
the Holy Spirit by placing her will in God's will and
saying, "Here am I, a handmaiden of the Lord; let
it be with me according to your words," so we must
also receive and accept Christ in faith. Then he will
also begin and complete his work in us.

3. The church has the key and authority to loose
and to bind as Christ has commanded, to exclude
the evil and to accept the repentant, so that this is
binding in heaven in accordance with the words of
Christ (Matt. 16:19).

4. Each should first count the cost carefully as to
what he has to give up. But he should not counsel
with flesh and blood. For those who would enter
God's service must be prepared to be attacked and
to die for the truth and for the name of Christ, if it
be God's will, by water, fire, or the sword. For now
we have house and shelter, but we do not know
what today or tomorrow will bring. Therefore no
one should join for the sake of good days. He who
is not prepared to endure evil and good with all
the believers and to accept as good whatever the
Lord gives and ordains should leave it alone. We
will not put pressure on anyone who does not join
of his own free will. We desire to persuade no one
with smooth words. It is not a matter of human
compulsion from without or within, for God wants
voluntary service. Whoever cannot do this with joy

Two doves,
Beiteddine Palace,
Lebanon

and to the delight of his soul should therefore leave it alone and remain in his former station.

5. No one should take this step for the sake of another – the wife for her husband's sake or the husband for his wife's sake, or the children for the sake of their parents. That would be in vain and built on sand. It cannot endure. Instead, each one should build on the rock, Christ, purely to please God alone; for each must bear his own burden on the day of judgment.

6. Each must submit to and follow brotherly warning, admonition, and discipline and must practice the same toward others in the house of God, so that no one may become co-guilty in the sins of another.

7. Each one should yield himself up in obedience to God and his church and not be obstinate or do only what he wants to do, but allow himself to be placed wherever it is seen to be necessary for the good of the church.

8. No one any longer owns anything, for each gives and surrenders himself to the Lord and his church with all that he has and can do, as it was in the first apostolic church, in which no one said of his goods that they were his own, but they had all things in common (Acts 4:32). This we hold to be the surest way and the most perfect foundation; we are well assured of this in our hearts.

9. We say this clearly to each one now in advance so that there is no obligation to return anything to anyone later: If anyone should enter on this way and then cannot continue and should wish to have what was his returned, let him stay away now, keep what is his, and leave us in peace. Our concern is not to get money and goods, but to win God-fearing hearts.

10. Whoever has had wrong dealings that are punishable in the world – be it that he is in debt or has cheated someone – or if anyone has got himself involved in matters of marriage or is engaged to be married, he must first straighten out all these matters. For if someone should hide any of these things from us and let himself be baptized and we should afterward learn about it, we would have to exclude him as one who did not come into the church rightly, but by falsehood. Therefore let each be warned.

Hutterian baptismal instruction (ca. 1528–1600) included in Johannes Waldner's *Taufbüchlein* (ca. 1800).

Olha Pilyuhina, *In Anticipation of Joyful Embrace*, handwoven natural-wool tapestry, 2020

A Cosmic Perfection

*My grandparents' marriage broke.
But they never broke faith with their
bond to one another.*

DORI MOODY

There are no beautiful surfaces without a terrible depth.
—Friedrich Nietzsche

I LIKE TO THINK that I touched Opa's beard, and could feel its fibers. But like everything about Opa, I'm not sure. Maybe this is a fabricated memory based on the black-and-white photo in family albums – the little girl in the picture is not me but my older sister. Of Opa, my dad's father, I know little. He died when I was seven, but his wife, my Oma Rose (pronounced Rosa, in the German way) outlived her husband by fourteen years, many of those as a member of my parents' household.

My grandparents were among the very first members of the Bruderhof, a community church founded in rural Germany as a response to the destruction of World War I. My grandfather, Manfried Kaiser, was known within the community as quirky and sometimes annoying. Partially deaf, he had a heart of

Manfried and Rose on their wedding day, 1930

gold and generally thought the best of others. But he was also eccentric and prone to rash decisions, and he tended to confuse those who were trying to help him. Although he made lifetime vows as a member of the Bruderhof in 1930, he left the community multiple times. And although he believed in marriage for life and deeply loved his wife, the mother of his seven children, he walked out on his family more than once.

They were reunited many times, but they lived the last decades of his life apart, at her insistence. What was the meaning of the vows they took, then, which came to such an end? Why did he put his family through so much pain? What really happened during his disappearances? Why, with so much good-faith effort from all involved, was there no healing in this life? These questions troubled me, setting me on a search of family archives and historical records.

MANFRIED WAS BORN IN 1900 INTO A THURINGIAN family not far from where Friedrich Nietzsche lived. Manfried grew to appreciate Nietzsche for calling out the decadence and decline of Western society. I appreciate Nietzsche for a different observation. In *The Birth of Tragedy*, Nietzsche profiles the Greek gods Apollo and Dionysus, both sons of Zeus. Apollo, who stood for light and order, was the favorite, while Dionysus was raised by the river nymphs. He enjoyed music and dancing, drinking and revelry, and has always been connected to madness. Dionysus was eventually murdered by the Titans out of jealousy, but he rose again, resurrected from his severed limbs. Nietzsche called Apollo the "art-shaper," the type of god who got things done. Dionysus, free-spirited and vulnerable, Nietzsche says represents the "non-plastic art of music." But in this Nietzsche firmly linked the opposite gods together.

This analogy may be extended. Imagine a world that is all law and order, or imagine a world that is only chaos. Singly each could inflict damage and pain, paired they may create vibrant community. Any human association needs Apollo's law and order, but it also needs the creativity – and, yes, the chaos and emotion – of Dionysus.

My grandfather was like Dionysus, vulnerable and free-spirited, and it was this temperament that led him to visit the Bruderhof in the winter of 1929. There, he met Rose Meyer, who had joined a few years earlier, and they became engaged.

Marriage vows on the Bruderhof were taken as seriously, and considered as permanent, as the lifetime vows of membership. Eberhard Arnold, leader and founder of the community, prepared Manfried and Rose for their wedding over the next full year, with much care. On March 2, 1930, Eberhard officiated the wedding; the text began with the Sumerian Lament of 2000 BC and ended with Revelation. One line stands out: "In the heavenly wedding of pure love, cosmic perfection reveals itself."

In their wedding photo Manfried and Rose stand looking toward the horizon. Manfried wrote he was "joyful beyond all his dreams."

Dori Moody is a Bruderhof member and an editor at Plough. *She lives with her husband at Danthonia, a Bruderhof community in New South Wales, Australia.*

THERE WERE PROBLEMS FROM THE BEGINNING.
Manfried's warm and cheerful outlook was
his strength, but his opinionated nature and
poor decision-making caused friction. After
a particularly difficult day in 1933, Manfried
and Rose were invited to speak to the other
members. Rose asked for prayers. She was
often quite desperate at home with her growing
family and unpredictable husband. Eberhard
urged compassion for "our dear Rose" and
understanding for Manfried, whose unfortunate
memory-clouding made him unreliable but
who "clearly has a good will and does his best to
radiate love and kindness." Eberhard exhorted
the fellow members to help lovingly carry the
challenges that Manfried and Rose faced as
individuals and as a couple. "We want to stand
faithfully by our Rose," he said, "and we want as
a church community to be completely open for
Manfried and to help him."

Manfried and Rose never forgot this pastoral
support. My grandfather loved the word
Gemeinde, which literally translates as "church,"
but for him it meant something more akin to
a church-brotherhood. His reverence for the
mystical body of the *Gemeinde* ran through
his very soul. For Manfried, being a lifetime
member of a church that admonished but also
forgave was being a part of a great whole. A
wholeness that encompassed even faults.

In 1934 my father Leonhard (always "Loni")
was born after two daughters, Detta and Rosie.
Filled with awe at the arrival of a son, Manfried
wrote to Eberhard with great cheer. Rose also
wrote, referencing a recent address Eberhard
had given entitled "The Root of Grace." In this
talk, he spoke of his own weaknesses and fail-
ings, the limitations of human power, and the
greatness of God: only when man relinquished
his own power could God work through him.
Rose, feeling very powerless already, desired to
find God's will in her vulnerability. It was clear

that life at home with a
new baby was not easy.

And then Manfried
took off. He was gone
for a few days.

Eberhard heard of
this departure, and he
wrote to Manfried and
Rose afterward, "It
was a difficult time for
you both when you,
dear Manfried, went
away so unexpectedly.
This pained me for
you and for all of us,
but I thank God that he protected you and
brought you back home." He suggested, "If
ever a dangerous heaviness comes over you
again, I expect you to come at once in trust
to me. When in earnest, the prayer of faith is
powerful."

Children of
Manfried and
Rose at the
Bruderhof
in Germany,
1935

AS THE 1930S WORE ON, TIMES BECAME VERY TOUGH
indeed. When the Nazi government closed the
community school in 1934 (an inspector was
shocked to discover the pupils hadn't been
taught any Nazi songs), the Bruderhof whisked
away the community's children to Liechtenstein
for schooling and refuge, including five-year-
old Detta. Family separation and extreme
poverty now faced all the members as National
Socialism made communal life more and more
difficult. Anxiety mounted at the possibility of
betrayal by local villagers. The strain of persecution and separation of family wore on the
Kaisers. Manfried's declining hearing didn't
work well with the need to whisper so as not be
overheard by unfriendly neighbors.

Manfried left again for a month. Eberhard's
care of the couple sustained them, and by
October 1935 Manfried was once again in good

Olha Pilyuhina, *Golden Birds*, handwoven natural-wool tapestry, 2019

standing as a member. But the hammer blows that ended the year were swift and shocking. Eberhard died unexpectedly on a dismal, cold November day after a failed surgery. In December, still reeling, Manfried and Rose lost their fourth child, Daniel Eberhard, only three hours after he was born. In the desolate cemetery, Manfried had said farewell twice, first to a great man of God, then to his own child who had not even lived one day. Small solace that their two graves were close together in the frozen ground.

The community, now lacking Eberhard's leadership, faced increasing sanctions from without, fatigue and discouragement from within. Then in September 1936, Manfried and other adult males were called to register for the German military. Manfried could not obtain a passport, so could not travel abroad. But in April 1937, just ten days before the German Bruderhof was dissolved by the Gestapo, the Kaiser family chanced traveling without passports toward an English Bruderhof. Now expecting their fifth child, the family took a train out of Germany and boarded a ship to Dover. By some fortuitous chance, they were allowed entrance. Manfried would never return to his German homeland.

When Rose gave birth to another girl, Sara Monika, that June, Manfried felt "God was a true friend" in sending this new, English-born daughter. Though they hadn't left all their troubles behind, their time in the Cotswolds was a respite after years of starvation and persecution. A spring day in May 1939 brought the joyful welcome of a baby brother, Paul Gerhardt.

But the peace didn't last. By the fall of 1939 anti-German sentiment ran so high that after England declared war on Germany on September 3, the German members of the Cotswold Bruderhof community had to appear before a tribunal and were ordered to remain within a five-mile radius of home, or be sent to internment camps.

Within weeks of this declaration, Manfried was picked up outside the radius. Why he was there was not clear. There are conflicting accounts. Some say he deliberately walked outside the zone to attract arrest, others that he wandered out by mistake. A fellow community member recalled that the road signs in the surrounding villages were intentionally changed to confound an invading German army, but in the end only confused a refugee. Manfried himself stated that he had experienced a breakdown.

His case was reviewed by a tribunal, but the record of what happened there remained buried for eight decades. Only now does a Freedom of Information inquiry with the British National Archives dispel some of the mystery.

On the back of the "Male Enemy Alien Internment Refugee" card, the judge in the case describes a refugee who "speaks practically no English, is intractable in camp, and is obviously mentally unstable. He may run away from camp again and professes his intention of doing so and has the idea that imprisonment transforms him into a martyr." (Manfried's "martyr" reference likely referred to 1935 meetings when Eberhard Arnold had admonished community members to be ready to stand up against the Nazi regime. Eberhard had recalled

About the artist: Olha Pilyuhina lives in Reshetylivka, Ukraine, where she contintues the regional tradition of tapestry-making, using time-honored technology and natural materials to create original artwork. Reflecting on the bird series accompanying this article, Pilyuhina says: "These are stories about love, trust, fidelity, and the movement of kindred souls to meet each other."

the Anabaptists of the Reformation era who had suffered imprisonment and death as martyrs for their faith; he urged community members to be ready for the same fate.)

The judge recommended against internment and raised the question of commitment to a mental hospital. But when, "in defiance of my warning yesterday," Manfried again went out of bounds, the judge sent him to be interned. He was not heard from again until February 1940, when he sent a disjointed note from his internment camp in southern England.

Back in the Cotswolds, the day of Manfried's disappearance came like destruction. Rose had to deal with all the unanswered questions, the reports from authorities, the bewilderment of her fellow church members, and the devastation of their children. Little Rosie cried night after night in panic and fear for the safety of her father. But in the light of day the perceptive child felt shame. What great crime had her father committed that police snatched him away from her?

On June 24, 1941, Manfried was sent with other German internees to the seaport of Liverpool. There the ocean liner *Duchess of York* took them to Canada. A similar convoy of internees had left Liverpool for Canada on July 2, 1940, aboard the *Arandora Star*, which was torpedoed and sunk by a German submarine off the Irish coast. Over half the 1,524 crew and passengers died. *The Duchess of York,* thankfully, arrived safely in Canada.

Of the next seven years in exile, Manfried never spoke.

ROSE AND HER CHILDREN DIDN'T STAY LONG ON English soil either. Due to increasing local hostility against the pacifist, German-speaking Bruderhof and reports of "enemy aliens" being rounded up, the Bruderhof decided to leave England. In March 1942, the rest of the family arrived in the Paraguayan jungle. There was at least some communication: five letters Rose wrote to her husband from Paraguay were preserved by a fellow internee, Hugo Brinkmann. Manfried must have shared the letters with Hugo, who transcribed them into his own diary. (Hugo, who became Manfried's closest friend, would himself join the Bruderhof after the war, introduced to it by these letters from Rose.)

Rose's first letter was dated August 28, 1941, almost two years after Manfried disappeared from the Cotswold community. Characteristically humble, she began with a wish for pardon for any hurt she may have caused him. She wrote of her wish that Manfried would return to his vocation, and be reinvigorated by the love he had felt when he joined the Bruderhof. Her last sentence: "So I ask you with heartfelt wishes for forgiveness, and I greet you with an old yet new love." Did my grandfather ever ask *her* for forgiveness? I don't know.

When I reread these letters, I feel the anguish of a wife missing her husband. She wrote great thoughts as if in answer to her own painful, smaller, and necessary thoughts of immediate survival. She had five children from two to ten years old to parent alone. She still grieved the loss of her fourth child; she wondered how her mother and siblings fared back in Germany. Rose stayed true to her vocation, but in the bitter battle against doubt and despair, peace disappeared along with her husband. It too seemed to be interned, somewhere far away.

Manfried wrote faithfully to Rose, but only one of his letters survives, a response to the suggestion from Bruderhof ministers that when released, he go first to a Hutterite colony in Canada (at the time the Bruderhof and the Hutterites were sister churches). Manfried agreed without reservation; nothing was too hard if in the end it led back to the

Gemeinde. But the letter's final sentence, "When will redemption come?" captures Manfried's deep loneliness.

By August 1943 Manfried had joined other internees allowed to work outside the camps for local Canadian farmers. The work outdoors afforded them a bit of freedom. Apparently, the overwhelming desire to be back with the *Gemeinde* bombarded Manfried's heart and mind so forcefully as to overcome all reason. Despite the fact that the nearest Hutterite colony was miles away, he decided to head in that direction, leaving behind a note explaining his intentions and destination. Once again he was on the run, absent without leave. He was recaptured just up the road. He could have been shot, but the Canadians were kind and patient. His punishment was not severe, but his days working on farms were over.

This episode was never part of family lore; I only learned about it thanks to a lead from a Canadian museum. As I picture it, all these years later, my heart feels like cheering him on: "Go, Opa, go!" Then I feel a sheepish chagrin at my reaction, for deep down I am pleased that nobody back at the Bruderhof is likely to have known that he had once again "run away." I am happy to share this little secret with Opa and the Canadian authorities.

ON MAY 8, 1945, THE INMATES OF THE CAMPS WERE called together for the announcement that Germany had surrendered and the war in Europe was over. One internee remembers the goodbye speech of their presiding camp

officer, who cautioned those leaving the relative peace and security of the camp that they would return to altered circumstances: "Remember when you go home your relationship has changed, and you have changed. You have been long apart."

All internees who had come from England were returned there first. Finally, in August, 1946, Manfried began the lengthy journey to Paraguay by way of Morocco. My image of him during a layover in Casablanca comes from the film by that name: I picture him walking past Rick's Café Américain with poignant scraps of Dooley Wilson's song trickling out into the street: "Woman needs man, and man must have his mate, that no one can deny." After seven years, Manfried was on his way to find his Rose.

For his long-anticipated arrival, the Kaiser family assembled with the rest of the community. Approximately two hundred members gathered in a big circle for the welcome. Loni strained to see the incoming wagon, and Paul Gerhardt jumped up and down. Two men were in the wagon: one tall and young, one aged and worn. "Run to your father; there is your father!" the community members exclaimed.

Manfried, *center row, far left,* at a POW camp in Canada, 1942

Loni and Paul Gerhardt, suddenly unsure, were propelled forward. Rosie, coming behind them, saw her brothers not knowing which newcomer to choose. They hugged the taller man, the wrong one. She saw her mother, overcome with shyness, remain in the background. Rosie went to her father, who seemed much smaller than she remembered. Manfried walked from one person to the next, shaking hands and looking deep into faces. He was home.

First came the miracle. Ten months after Manfried's return to Rose, very early on July 25, 1948, a baby girl was born. Manfried woke up Rosie to tell her the joyful news. Phoebe Elfriede Kaiser, nine years younger than Paul Gerhardt, was the baby her siblings had long dreamed of.

Then came the reality. A new father again at forty-eight, Manfried felt much older. He couldn't hear well at all, and often had severe headaches. Meanwhile, Rose was impatient for him to catch on to being a family man. After seven years, surrounded only by men, he had lost the knack of being around women and children. Trouble with home life mirrored community life. The *Gemeinde*, having struggled through a decade of poverty, harsh climate, and terrible world events, was not how Manfried remembered it.

Over the next decade the couple tried to reclaim the lost years. There was little professional help available for the hearing problems Manfried endured, or the mental anguish they both suffered.

During one of these periods, my father's friend taught him chess, a passion he would eventually share with me. In chess, a situation in which one is obliged to make a disadvantageous move is called zugzwang. It almost always means the loss of a key piece, and often defeat. Zugzwang sums up the state of the Kaiser family during those years; keeping the marriage together appeared doomed.

IN 1956 THE GERMAN GOVERNMENT PASSED A LAW allowing for federal compensation for victims of National Socialism. Manfried, Rose, Detta, and my father all lodged claims. Manfried's claim was misplaced (this is so characteristic I am hardly surprised), but the other claims were with my family records – I pore over the records for weeks, translating and collecting information. In the end though, the amounts don't really matter. Who can price human suffering? Money cannot purchase forgiveness or closure, and I find myself angry once again at men and governments long dead. Then I discover something.

Mistakenly attached as the last document of my father's seventy-five-page record, there is a typed page of notes from Manfried's lost file. Here I learn which illness caused his deafness, and a potential contributor to his eccentric behavior over the years.

In 1925, years before he met my grandmother, Manfried had been hospitalized in Hamburg with "brain fever." The record states: "Since then, progressive bad hearing with tinnitus, and headaches." Likely this was encephalitis, a serious condition causing lingering aftereffects, like headaches, seizures, and memory loss, even psychosis. His physical and mental infirmities were no one's fault. But the pain they brought about was the birth of his and my family's tragedy.

Whatever the cause of human frailty, the question becomes: What is to be done? Nietzsche described the life of the *übermensch* (superman) as the way for man to rise above a fallen state; man was doomed to fail unless he could generate superhuman qualities.

Olha Pilyuhina, *Fidelity*, handwoven natural-wool tapestry, 2020

Rose Kaiser,
early 1980s

Eberhard Arnold advocated for the opposite. Where Nietzsche bemoaned the state of being "all too human," Eberhard held that being human was no shame, provided this vulnerability led to reliance on the power of God. To Eberhard, Jesus was the *übermensch*, the man who rose above.

Like my grandfather, Nietzsche experienced significant mental infirmity toward the end of his life, and even came to sign his letters "Dionysus." His brilliance and will to power could not save him from a lonely and desperate end.

In the fall of 1953, seven years after Manfried's return, my grandparents separated for good. Rose moved to a different Bruderhof community, and never lived again under the same roof as her husband. This final separation came after much effort, from within the family and without. Was Nietzsche, not Eberhard, correct? God had seemingly not answered their prayers with healing.

Manfried never gave up hope of reuniting with his wife. In a letter in March 1955, around their twenty-fifth anniversary, Manfried again wrote to "My dearest Rose!" He simply greeted her with love because he could not visit her in person.

Rose always worked hard, and seldom complained. But her soul hurt. After almost twenty years in Paraguay, she went back to Germany in 1961, to visit her mother and brother Willi in Dresden. Willi had tuberculosis and looked aged and worn; his wife and two children, of Jewish descent, had

been exterminated in the Holocaust. Her brother Gerhard had also died in the war. There was the happiness of reunion, but also the extreme sadness of memory and loss. Rose's hometown was in ruins, her family shattered.

Recognizing her fragile mental state, a Bruderhof community doctor accompanied Rose to a psychiatric hospital, where she was treated for six weeks. Her psychiatrists observed that she was "under special burdens" and "prone to paranoid reactions."

The special burdens that Rose carried were so myriad, I marvel that her life did not end here, in 1961, at the age of fifty-seven. But she lived another thirty-four years. I cannot say her burdens disappeared. I hesitate to speak of healing. One's spirit can be broken beyond complete repair. Stories of resilience and the indomitable human spirit might happen in other families, but that didn't happen in mine. But the largest burden Rose carried, the burden of perceived failure, did heal.

MANFRIED'S LIFE WAS IN PIECES. THE DEATHS OF his spiritual father and a baby son weighed on him, and now his wife was gone too. He was chopped down, reduced. What wholeness can rise from such brokenness? What does it mean for Dionysus to rise with life in his dismembered limbs?

On his sixtieth birthday, Manfried wrote, "In the beginning, I was often angry about my desperate surroundings." From these depths, he decided: "So I look to the greatness of the cause, and will only serve love, not anger." He concluded, "Humble, I must remain." His decision to turn from anger and set his heart on humility was the path of Eberhard Arnold, who thirty years before had bequeathed to Manfried and Rose a great gift – the guidance to strive downward, to dismantle human power, to surrender everything to Jesus.

This surrender had started long ago in another vow. Manfried and Rose had both been baptized as adults, my grandmother before she joined the community, and my grandfather by Eberhard Arnold. Their baptismal vows to God provided a foundation in their lives, binding them to "the fellowship of believers." Many times over the years, this link would give them something solid to stand on.

Manfried with a grand-daughter, the author's sister, in 1974

THE LAST DECADES OF MY GRANDPARENTS' LIVES were similar. Both were joyful members of the *Gemeinde.* Manfried gardened, sang, read voraciously, and hand-lettered "psalms" or poems for people he loved. Rose gardened, knitted, and when asked to by her grandchildren, juggled. The sad parts of the past fell away.

Opa Manfried lived eighty-one years and died surrounded by his children. He was buried on Good Friday, April 15, 1981. His wife Rose could not bring herself to attend the funeral, but listened to the service by telephone from her home, a Bruderhof community two hours distant. My aunt Rosie, grieving his loss, additionally felt deep pain for her estranged parents. When she returned after the funeral, she did not know how to relay the experience to her mother. She felt unable to share about the holy victory that surrounded her father's last hours. Manfried had run to his final destination. He was home at last.

When I read Aunt Rosie's memoirs about this day I cannot hold back my own tears, which splash down onto my collected notes. I brush the tears away angrily, for I am suddenly upset. But toward whom? Whose fault is it anyway? Then I am silent, strangely comforted in the knowledge that Opa was buried on a Good Friday. And I do not dare to speak of justice to the Father of the Crucified on Good Friday.

AS THE DISMEMBERMENT of Dionysus ends with rebirth, so too is Good Friday not the end. My own baptismal vows, taken just weeks before my grand-mother's death in 1995, hang on the timeless assurance that resurrection crowns sorrow, that cosmic perfection will be revealed.

Somewhere during my research I read that up to 80 percent of the men who returned from Canadian internment after World War II experienced failed relationships. Whether or not that is true, Manfried's marriage to Rose did not survive those years of separation. Even a loving church could not patch together their disrupted union. The *Gemeinde,* after all, does not make people perfect. But it did continue to hold them when their human strength came to an end.

The six surviving children of Manfried and Rose all chose lives of commitment to the same Christian community their parents had joined. Those who married have been faithful in those marriages, and a dozen grandchildren have started families of their own. Manfried and Rose's many descendants, including myself and my children, are grateful for the imperfect union that gave us life and for the community of the *Gemeinde.* We laugh together often. But when trials come along that are no laughing matter, we recall the confidence of those who loved intensely, believed always, and trusted that God would intervene when life placed them in zugzwang. ❧

Olha Pilyuhina, *I Fly to You*, handwoven natural-wool tapestry, 2020

Can Love Take Sides?

The law of love excludes no one, but requires a choice from everyone.

WENDELL BERRY

When advocating for justice in public life, it's easy to think we're championing the side of love against the side of hate. But that's not love, Wendell Berry argues in the following book excerpt:

I RECOMMEND SECOND THOUGHTS about the possibility of a "side" of love, but current political rhetoric tends toward such an absolute division. The side of hate is composed of avowed racists; avowed racists have espoused an absolute, un-excepting prejudice against a kind of people; and so they may be called "the side of hate" rightly enough. That haters hate is morally as straightforward and uncomplicated as it can be. But they themselves are perceived by the side of love as a kind of people. And the side of love, as perceived by the side of hate, is a kind of people also, another kind. And so we have a confrontation of two opposite kinds of people, lovers and haters, each side as absolute in its identity as it can make itself, and they do not know each other. They cannot imagine each other. For the haters, this situation is wonderfully simple and entirely acceptable. They don't need even a notion of consequence. They are there to oppose. That is all. The lovers, on the contrary, have everything at stake and the situation is clouded by moral danger.

Because the confrontation is between two categories of people who do not know each other, it will be easy for the side of love first to understand love merely as opposite and

Dean Mitchell, *American in Black and White*, acrylic, 2017

Wendell Berry is an American novelist, poet, essayist, environmental activist, cultural critic, and farmer.

opposed to hate, and then to generalize this opposition as an allegorical battle of Love versus Hate, exchanging slogan for slogan, gesture for gesture, shout for shout. Then if nature and the rule of battle go unchecked, the side of love begins to hate the side of hate. And then the lovers are defeated, for they have defeated themselves. They have fallen into the sort of trap that Mr. Jefferson set for, among others, himself. If you say, "All men are created equal," then adding

Love that hates has canceled itself. It cannot survive its hatred of hate any more than one can survive minus one.

"except for some," the exception overturns the rule, and a great deal else along with it. Just so, love that hates has canceled itself. It cannot survive its hatred of hate any more than one can survive minus one. It is no more. Chaos and old night have come again.

With us, love has been reduced mostly to a popular word, easy to use to intensify a frivolous appreciation. "Oh, I *love* it!" we say when told of something really cute. Or it can be used as a handy weapon against the haters of whom we disapprove. Too bad. But love comes into our civilization – the Gospels being the source best known to me – as a way of being in the world. It is a force, extraordinarily demanding and humbling, dangerous too, for those who attempt to take it seriously.

As a force and a way of being, love is never satisfied with partiality. It is compelled, by its own nature and logic, to be always trying to make itself whole. This is why the Sermon on the Mount tells us to love our enemies. That is an unconditional statement. It does not tell us to fight our enemies in order to improve them or convert them by our love.

In practice, this commandment seems to cancel or delete "enemy" as a category of thought.

MY LONG ADVOCACY began in love and fear for my own home country and community. By the time I was thirty, I could see that my native place and the life of it, along with my affection for it, was not in favor with the urban-industrial system that had clouded over it after World War II. Such a place – rural, small, "backward," and "under-developed" – was, in fact, invisible, virtually nonexistent, to that system, and thus mortally endangered by it. I could see that, as it was, its days were numbered. But I could see also that, as it was, its human community was taking respectable care of itself and of the local countryside that supported it. It was clear to me that this good keeping, if it could survive and be cherished, held the possibility of better keeping. There was nothing in the dominant economy and state of mind, however, that would support such a possibility – let alone the possibility that anything at all in such a place, or in fact in any place, might be cherished.

My concern might reasonably have made me an advocate for "soil conservation." But I was a native. My affection for my place was already established in my heart and unspecialized. It included the people and other creatures along with the soil, and it has become ever clearer to me that you cannot conserve the land unless you can conserve the people who depend on the land, who care for it, and who know how to care for it – the people on whom the land depends.

Without quite knowing what I was doing at that time, I had entered the way of love and taken up its work. It could not be simplified or shortcut, but became ever more inclusive, complex, and difficult. Any violence that intrudes between the land and the people

extends its damage both ways. But I could not restrict my understanding of the problem of violence to my own place and people. Violence to one place cannot be dissociated from violence to any place. Violence to some people cannot be dissociated from violence to other people. This is the sort of difficulty that imposes an irremediable amateurism. I finally understood this and approved of it. It meant that my permanent motive would be love; it certainly did not mean that I was a hobbyist. But my commitment was pushing me way beyond my schooling. I would have to deal

with issues of science, of art, of religion, of economy, of ecology, and so on, with no fore-seeable limit. There can be no set bounds to the work of love when it faces boundless violence.

I am not speaking here of the love that thrives only by feeding upon a commensurate hatred, but rather of the love, perhaps more fearful, that draws no boundary around itself.

How might we imagine imposing by mere law the principles of equality and justice and love upon a society dominated in its economic life by the violent principles of individualism, competition, and greed? How might we imagine

Dean Mitchell, *Sunday Morning*, acrylic, 2017

the loyalty or patriotism that could protect the life of the land and the people of any place under the economic rule of "maximum force relentlessly applied"? What must we do for the success of the personal generosity, the common decency, the good manners that are the ultimate safeguards of equality and justice, now

If you see the world's goodness and beauty, and if you love your own place in it, then your love itself will be one of your life's great rewards.

that we apparently have settled into permanent war as the basis of our economy? Our economy, let us not forget, defines "equality" as the "right" of everybody to be as wasteful, violent, destructive, consumptive, lazy, and luxurious as everybody else.

For me, the greatest, most comprehensive difficulty, the one I endlessly return to, is that I do not think of the chattel slavery of the antebellum South as a problem that is isolatable or unique. The more I have read and thought about our history, and the more I have observed of the works and effects of our present economy, the more plainly I have seen that old-time version of slavery as one of a continuum of violent exploitations, including other forms of slavery, that has been with us since the European discovery of America. It is so far our history's dominant theme.

A failing too little remembered but nonetheless significant is that the southern planters, using slave labor, cropped their land to exhaustion. The availability of apparently endless tracts of "new" land to the west made the eastward lands dispensable. And so we come to a key word in the story of American development or progress: Anything superabundant or "inexhaustible" can be treated as *dispensable*.

One of the cruelest ironies of postbellum history is that emancipation, in freeing the slaves of white proprietorship, freed them also from their market value and made them individually worthless in the "free" economy – like the poor whites whose "free labor" was already abundantly available, and who thus were individually dispensable.

So far, there has been no limit to this equation between apparent abundance and dispensability. The immigrants who work in Tyson's meat factories, where they are ruthlessly exposed to the coronavirus (among other dangers) are extremely poor, having only their bodily labor to depend on; they also are numerous and therefore are considered dispensable. We must remember also the homegrown great corporations that depend upon, and defend, forced labor in China. But this freedom to enslave, use, and use up is not limited to corporations. Because the atmosphere is so far too abounding to be captured and sold, it also is worthless, useful for disposing of wastes. All of us now pollute it freely, at no cost except to the health of every living thing.

On the contrary: It seems natural to me to think that there is a law of love operating in this world. If you see the world's goodness and beauty, and if you love your own place in it (no deed or title required), then your love itself will be one of your life's great rewards. That is the law that rules the "sticker," the settler, the actual patriot. The opposite law is that of greed, which sees the goodness and beauty of the world as wealth and power. It says: Take what you want. No individual person is purely a settler or an exploiter, but perhaps every person must submit to the rule of one law or the other. ⤐

Editors' Picks

What Your Food Ate
How to Heal Our Land and Reclaim Our Health

David R. Montgomery and Anne Biklé
(W. W. Norton)

Carrots and spinach are generally agreed to be good for you. And my mind hasn't changed on that. But after reading *What Your Food Ate*, by husband-wife science duo David Montgomery and Anne Biklé, I've found myself paying a lot more attention to their source, the soil they came from, because, as Biklé and Montgomery show, human health and soil health are deeply intertwined.

In the early twentieth century, Sir Albert Howard, a British soil scientist, became convinced that traditional farmers in India utilizing compost generated not only healthier but also more healthful crops. His book *The Soil and Health* went on to influence writers like Wendell Berry. Howard's contemporary Lady Eve Balfour came to the similar conclusion that it was the life of the soil – the microscopic fungi and bacteria – that helped make healthy and nutritious plants. According to Montgomery and Biklé, she concluded that "healthy soil was a recipe for healthy people" and "even went so far as to call for hospitals to retain soil scientists on staff." Balfour and Howard were rejected by the scientific consensus of their day, not because of a lack of evidence for their position, but because it didn't fit with the model of progress that posited chemically-based agriculture as the way of the future.

We are now facing the consequences of that progress. An emphasis on crop yields at any cost has depleted our soils and left our food far less nutritious than it was in the time of Howard and Balfour. Studies now show up to "40 percent declines in the mineral content of fruits and vegetables over the previous half-century." Broccoli alone has seen its calcium "decreased by about two-thirds from 1950 to 2003." The consequences of these reductions are legion and Biklé and Montgomery spend much of the book tracing those results and their remedies.

Their solution is a form of agriculture that centers on soil health rather than a pure increase in yields: more compost and less tillage. The authors visit a variety of farmers, from no-till vegetable growers to pasture-based ranchers, to show how building soil life increases the nutrition of food. Food that is rich in micronutrients and phytochemicals also tastes better; flavor, if we learn to interpret it rightly, can be a good guide to health.

Montgomery and Biklé end their book with an almost religious fervor. "Soil not only feeds us today but will feed our children's children, and this calls for some reverence," they write. A humble care for the soil gets to the heart of who we are as human beings. It is no accident that both in English and in Hebrew our substance is defined in terms of the soil – the human from the humus, the *adam* (human) from the *adamah* (agricultural soil). Our lives have always been intertwined with the life of the soil. *What Your Food Ate* is a brilliant and engaging call to be humus-beings once more and to live with care for the least of our creaturely neighbors, the living soil upon which our wholeness depends.

—*Ragan Sutterfield, author,*
Wendell Berry and the Given Life

The Last White Man
A Novel

Mohsin Hamid
(Riverhead Books)

British-Pakistani novelist Mohsin Hamid is known for fiction that uses surrealist premises to explore issues including migration, religious extremism, and race. In *The Last White Man*, Hamid draws on his personal experiences of being subjected to the white gaze after 9/11 to imagine a world where whiteness transforms to brown. The end result is an unsettling fairy tale that does not quite live up to the ambitions of its premise, but is interesting nonetheless.

> **Absent a metaphysics that sees everyone as created in the image of God, personal experience becomes the sum total of the self.**

When Anders, the novel's protagonist, first awakens to discover he has transformed from white to "a deep and undeniable brown," he is filled with "an unexpected, murderous rage" at this theft of himself. He calls in sick from work, visits the grocery store, smokes pot, and then finally works up the courage to call his lover, Oona. As the story unfolds, additional white people undergo this transformation, resulting in social upheaval in the nameless town of the nameless country in which none of the characters have surnames. Oona's mother, radicalized by radio stations, describes the events as "the plot against their kind" and praises the newly forming white militias. Pizza delivery becomes a two-person job, one to deliver the pizza and the other to stand guard with a pistol. Along with these unnerving changes to the social world, the omniscient narrator tells us, the days become shorter and cooler and "the leaves no longer as confident in their green," adding an aura of menace to the natural and unremarkable turn of the season.

In recent decades, the aspiration to be color-blind regarding race has been critiqued both because it is seen as impossible and because it ignores ongoing effects of systemic racism. Hamid's novel sidesteps these critiques by flattening the racial diversity of its characters entirely. The narrator tells us the new world of universalizing brown leads to one form of blindness – difficulty recognizing people you previously knew – but also a new sensitivity to voice and facial expression. This seems to be the normative thrust of the book: race is constructed and ought not be salient; what matters is the human underneath.

But it is in raising the question of the human underneath that the book falters. After his transformation, Anders initially feels that "under the surface it was still him," but then realizes that the way people interact with you "changes what you are, who you are." The ending of the book suggests that it is our loving relationships with others that define us. Certainly this is a better basis for identity than the faulty metaphysics of race, but what of the soul?

Absent a metaphysics that sees everyone as created in the image of God, personal experience becomes the sum total of the self, and also the basis for ethics. Thus, Anders's father can overcome prejudice once his own son is transformed, and Oona's mother can affirm her daughter's intimacy with a dark man after both she and her daughter become dark as well. This metaphysics may work well enough in the fantastical world of Hamid's novel, but in our own decidedly less abstract world, a deeper metaphysics is required.

—*Anthony M. Barr, Philadelphia*

Untrustworthy

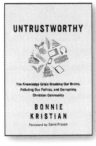

Bonnie Kristian
(Brazos Press)

Bonnie Kristian, formerly an editor at *The Week* and *Christianity Today*, opens her most recent book, *Untrustworthy*, with a sweeping claim: "American society has a knowledge crisis, and the American church is no exception." As the subtitle of her book plainly states, this crisis is "breaking our brains, polluting our politics, and corrupting Christian community."

Presently, there's no shortage of attention being paid to the societal ills attributed to social media and the adverse consequences of misinformation. Often, however, these criticisms are too narrow in scope, focusing only on major social media platforms and construing complex social phenomena as merely technical problems that could be managed through regulation, policy tweaks, or better content moderation. Kristian takes a broader view of the situation, examining, for example, how traditional media have also contributed to the crisis.

The book has a chapter on the growing prevalence of conspiracists, grounded in Kristian's reporting on QAnon over the past few years, and one on the plight of expertise in an age of information superabundance – a case of "democratized knowledge, public hubris." In each chapter, she provides insights into how our capacity to seek the truth is derailed by an inability to think constructively beyond the bounds of our tribe and our experience, respectively. Along the way, Kristian takes readers through the fraught territory of "cancel culture" and what, following Matt Bruenig, she calls "identitarian deference."

Though Kristian is sensitive to the ways in which social media has exacerbated and channeled these developments, she is careful not to reduce her argument to a critique of specific platforms. In the digital "public sphere," a multitude of existing communities, each with its distinct culture and norms, has been thrust together within systems that, it turns out, are not particularly conducive to mutual understanding and respect. The priests and prophets of digital technology promised that increased connection would lead to a form of cultural unity. Instead, as Marshall McLuhan anticipated, the "global village" is a place of "arduous interfaces and abrasive situations."

Kristian's closing chapters invite readers to consider how we might interact with this new information ecosystem more virtuously. Here she provides sound and sane counsel, and a welcome reminder that we bear some responsibility for learning how to navigate it. As Kristian puts it, "We've spent forty years dramatically increasing how much information the average person encounters daily, and we've made no effort to equip ourselves to handle that shift."

But a focus on virtue is susceptible to the charge of inadequacy. Is it realistic or wise to pit personal virtue against problems of such scale and scope? Can we expect public knowledge to lead to understanding and solidarity while our encounters with the world and those we share it with are so profoundly structured and mediated by digital technologies that have clearly led us not together but apart? While we sort out those questions, Kristian has given readers a helpful set of practices and strategies with which to meet, even if just provisionally, one of the biggest challenges of our age.

—*L. M. Sacasas, author,*
The Convivial Society

The Raceless Gospel

Half a century after his death, Clarence Jordan still has much to teach America about war, wealth, race, and religion.

STARLETTE THOMAS

Clarence Jordan was a Southern Baptist pastor and farmer who, in 1942, founded Koinonia Farm, an interracial, pacifist communal experiment on depleted farmland in Americus, Georgia. The latest book in the Plough Spiritual Guides series, The Inconvenient Gospel: A Southern Prophet Tackles War, Wealth, Race, and Religion *(October 2022) offers a selection of Jordan's talks and writings. To introduce the book, we asked Starlette Thomas, a Baptist minister, what Jordan's message means to her.*

B EFORE YOU READ *The Inconvenient Gospel* and enter the life of Clarence Jordan through his own words, it's worth taking stock of where Christianity in North America finds itself these days, more than half a century after his death.

You might be as puzzled as I am. Didn't Jesus call himself "the way"? How hard could it be for his disciples to keep their eyes on him, to keep walking straight in the way he showed us? Turns out his way is also pretty narrow, and few find it (Matt. 7:14).

Artwork by Julie Lonneman. Used by permission.

Hyperpoliticized and evenly divided on who's wrong and who's right, the North American church continues to toe "the color line." Not much has changed in five decades: we're still segregated at 11 a.m. on Sunday. The sociopolitical construct of race still holds the reins, controlling the ways in which Christian communities of faith are formed in most places. We still avoid talking about race, but we'll sing in a well-meaning way: "Jesus loves the little children, all the children of the world. Red and yellow, black and white, they are precious in his sight."

But that's not how Jesus loves the little children. It is well past time that we deracialize his gospel, as his love is not color-coded. God's love is unconditional, which means it is uncategorical.

Besides, we're not supposed to see our bodies that way. Paul wrote to the believers at Corinth: "Even though we once knew Jesus from a human point of view, we know him no longer in that way. So, if anyone is in Christ, there is a new creation: everything old has passed away; see, everything has become new!" (2 Cor. 5:16–17). Or as Clarence Jordan put it in "The Priceless Knowledge in Clay Pots: The Second Letter to the Atlanta Christians": "That's why, from here on out, we pay absolutely no attention to a person's outward appearance. It is true that we once knew Christ physically, but now we do so no longer. Therefore, if a man is a Christian he is a brand-new creation. The old guy is gone: look, a new man has appeared."

To be clear, this call for a raceless gospel is not a suggestion that we be colorblind, and it is not a vision of what some have described as a post-racial society. Instead, it is an invitation to see race as it really is: a caste system with a good paint job. This raceless gospel is also a proclamation of an undivided "kin-dom" to come. Until then, we should see race as the good news of socially colored white skin and therefore "another gospel" (Gal. 6–9). In *Cotton Patch Parables for Liberation,* Clarence Jordan writes, "The church of God does not respect color lines." But Jordan didn't just write it down; he lived it out, "precept upon precept, line upon line" (Isa. 28:13).

Clarence and Florence Jordan, with Martin and Mabel England and a few others, drew a line in the sand at Koinonia Farm in Americus, Georgia, in 1942. Right then, not waiting for a more appropriate time, they bore witness to the hospitality, kinship, and fellowship of Christ's body. Jordan said, "Faith is not belief in spite of the evidence, but a life in scorn of the consequences." Academically trained and ordained, he knew what he was talking about. But his farmer's hands called him to do some deep digging in American soil foreign to this kind of Christian witnessing. As he worked the land, he toiled with the issues of race and its progeny as a spiritual discipline. It was important for Jordan that he lived it, that he brought it home, even though it was inconvenient.

Jordan called Koinonia Farm his "demonstration plot," where he dared to erase "the color line" by integrating his faith and his life, practicing it in community with African Americans, those socially colored black. It was forbidden, this so-called race-mixing, and he no doubt crossed the line. He got the Ku Klux Klan's attention and the group paid him several visits, firing bullets as they drove by. But Jordan kept his head down, and his head was on straight; he was a pacifist who founded a desegregated community because he was grounded in his faith. He saw that

Julie Lonneman, *Clarence Jordan,* 2020

Starlette Thomas is director of The Raceless Gospel Initiative at Good Faith Ministries and host of the Raceless Gospel *podcast.*

the American church was following in the footsteps of the American empire, and he went another way.

Perhaps Jordan had a vision like that of Peter, who reported back to the New Members Committee of the church at Jerusalem: "The Spirit told me to go with them and not to make a distinction between them and us" (Acts 11:12). Despite the disapproval of his neighbors, who cut ties and boycotted the farm, Jordan kept on digging and planting seeds in hopes that the church would change. He showed that you don't need much to make a difference.

Clarence Jordan didn't wait on the laws to change; instead, he followed the laws of Christ.

We are all God's children. What a shame it is that much of the North American church has chosen an Enlightenment idea about identity over the truth that we are all created in the image of God. Coloring in the face of God in peach tones, we have framed the divine in 11 x 17 and hung up an idolized version of ourselves in our homes and sanctuaries.

Careful not to change a thing, it seems that the North American church is, by and large, stuck in a time past, or perhaps walking back on its calling to be the reconciling body of Christ. Christianity is not following its leader. This is not a new insight but a necessary confession. From Jesus' first handpicked disciples until now, Christian believers have been a walking contradiction, with Jesus saying one thing and his followers doing another. These discrepancies have caused many Christians and onlookers to question whether the church is the right body for the job. Because it needs bodywork.

I found Clarence Jordan's words when I was looking at Christianity, realizing that in remaining segregated on Sunday mornings, it wasn't just missing something, but missing the point. In Jordan, I stumbled upon a guide who knew exactly where I expected my faith to take me, who shared my convictions, and whose faith had led him to defy the status quo. A Greek-reading green thumb, Clarence Jordan stuck out to me. I couldn't unsee the cotton patch evidence.

Jordan didn't wait on the world to change. Instead, he changed the world around him. He didn't wait on the laws to change; instead, he followed the laws of Christ. He lived in his own world, which proved to me that there is life outside of and apart from this racialized reality. It could be done, and I didn't have to wait on the North American church to do it. No, I could put my hands to the plow and turn my corner of the world upside down.

You may be wondering how my connection to Clarence Jordan came about, how a twenty-first-century African-American pastor finds herself enthusing about a Jim Crow-era Southern Baptist minister. You could say we were brought together by the Holy Spirit and a shared commitment to building community. A few years ago, I received a pastoral study grant from the Louisville Institute in Kentucky, supported by the Lilly Endowment, to take a sabbatical and undertake a deep dive into Clarence Jordan's life and writings.

At the time, I was questioning my faith in race and in the North American expression of Christianity, which supports it, evidenced by the fact that its churches come in black and white. Today, I have no doubt that American Christianity is complicit in oppression due to its silent, even unwitting, trading in the perks and privileges of white supremacy. I am not alone; there have always been Christians who sensed that the church was not living up to its

confessions, that it had somehow lost its way, that it would need witnesses who could shine a light when the church hid its own light for power, position, or material gain.

Christians in America must answer for the many ways that they do not identify with the way of Jesus or answer his call for justice. Far too many are wishy-washy, fifty-fifty, feigning laryngitis and pretending they cannot find their voice to answer the blood calling from the ground. Still, I must ask: Were you there for sweet Elijah McClain, who went to the store for snacks but never made it back home? Were you there for Ahmaud Arbery, stopped in his tracks while jogging? Were you there when they shot Breonna Taylor in her own home after midnight? Were you there when they choked the life out of George Floyd? When bowed heads at Mother Emanuel AME Church were filled with bullets? When supermarket shoppers in Buffalo, New York, were murdered in the aisles? Because if we aren't there for them, then why are we here? If these deaths don't affect you personally, how can we talk about being one nation, let alone the one body of Christ?

Word made flesh, Jesus is God on the ground, on the move, where the injustice is. Jesus is in the thick of it. Jesus is God face to face, in places we think he wouldn't be

caught dead and with the last people we would picture him with. As his disciples, we should be close on his heels and always be found in his company – no matter who he is keeping company with.

Unfortunately, instead of being known for "sharing all things in common" as the first Christians were, American Christians are known for shoving select scriptures down people's throats. Nauseated by this and no longer wanting to be associated with the likes of such Christians, many followers of Jesus

Clarence Jordan, *right*, at Koinonia Farm

The Inconvenient Gospel
A Southern Prophet Tackles War, Wealth, Race, and Religion

Clarence Jordan
Edited by Frederick L. Downing

The radical vision of the founder of Koinonia Farm, where Black and White Christians in Jim Crow Georgia pooled land and money to create "a demonstration plot for the kingdom of God."

plough.com/inconvenientgospel

You and the Koinonia Community have been in my prayers
continually for the last several months. The injustices and
indignities that you are now confronting certainly leave you in
trying moments. I hope, however, that you will gain consolation
from the fact that in your struggle for freedom and a true
Christian commmunity you have cosmic companionship. God grant
that this tragic midnight of man's inhumanity to man will soon
pass and the bright daybreak of freedom and brotherhood will
come into being.

Yours very truly,
M. L. King, Jr.,
Minister

Text from a letter dated February 8, 1957, from Martin Luther King Jr. to Clarence Jordan

have left the church building and are looking for him elsewhere. They know that he is found in community: at shared tables, at sickbeds, and at gravesides; with tortured souls; with those who secretly are interested yet don't want to be seen with him; with women and children.

For years, I had searched for a conversation partner who could double as a witness to this gnawing, nagging yearning for authentic being and belonging in Christian community – without the surveillance of race. I wanted to be seen fully, freely, and authentically, apart from "the white gaze." I needed to prove that it could be done, not just personally but in community. For me, that witness was Clarence Jordan. He made me believe again that there could be more to human being and belonging.

So, as part of my project, which looked at the malformation of Christian community due to the sociopolitical construct of race, I studied Clarence Jordan's writings and his witness at Koinonia Farm. I wanted to know more about the man who broke the laws of segregation to keep the law of love, which Jesus distilled for us in the Greatest Commandment, to "love your neighbor as yourself" (Matt. 22:39).

On Koinonia Farm's seventy-fifth anniversary, I walked the grounds and stood just outside Clarence Jordan's writing shack. I pictured him writing there. I wanted to be close to him, close to someone who kept their convictions even closer. My feet were dug in by then. I looked around and took in his handiwork, pecans on the ground ready to be harvested. His Christian identity was not a card he carried but a role he carried out and acted out in the world, and quite literally planted in the ground.

These observations led me to believe that the churches in North America will either be communal or coffins. There is no life in spaces cut off from entire communities. Churches will either be inclusive or invisible to generations who have no interest in hand-me-down hatreds, exclusionary prejudices, and sacred stereotypes. Going to these churches will make no difference if they offer the same selections and preferences as American society at large.

There is a generation that wants to see something different. And we are willing to go to the ends of the earth, and back in time, to find those who know the way – a way out of racialized identities and hierarchical forms of belonging in a capitalist society. For me and for many others, Clarence Jordan is one of those. A patron saint of community-builders, he still speaks to those who feel called to defy race and its categorized way of living. He inspires us to lay to rest this segregated expression of church and demonstrate a better way. ➤

Vole photograph by slowmotiongli. Used by permission.

Vows in Brief

How three monogamous animal couples got from courtship to "I do."

PHIL CHRISTMAN

RODENTS ARE HAVING A MOMENT. Look in any trendy restaurant – no, a little further down – and you may find rats. Guinea pigs overwhelm Gotham's animal shelters; a rare beaver even surprised passersby on the Williamsburg Bridge this spring. Looking beyond the city, if we must, we find mice accused of spreading Omicron and "squirrel roundups" in California.

Amongst such heady company, some rodents keep a lower profile. Two prairie voles – North Americans may know them by a somewhat vulgar nickname, "field mice," though their family name, *Microtus ochrogaster*, is perfectly respectable, and followed them from the Old World – mated for life last Saturday, under a bit of leafy covering in the backyard of a particularly tony Lincoln Park,

Phil Christman teaches first-year writing at the University of Michigan and is the editor of the Michigan Review of Prisoner Creative Writing.

Plough Quarterly • *Autumn 2022*   109

Kirk's Dik-Dik photography by Anushka Wijesinha. Used by permission.

Chicago, house. The happy couple already expects their first litter of five.

The parents of the groom are successful tunnel-builders. Their son attracted some local notoriety early last week when he departed from the community to take up and mark a circular bit of territory with his urine. All day Friday he defended this prime bit of real estate with all the tenacity of the NIMBY homeowners he shares a habitat with, chattering his teeth and raising his forefeet aggressively at no fewer than six would-be usurpers.

His bride-to-be was cagier. For a night and most of a day, she ignored his courtship displays to concentrate on her successful career as a burrower and disrupter of root systems. But there was just something about the scent of his pheromones, and after twenty-four hours, she found that his secretions had driven her mad with love. They reconnected. The several-day mating rut that followed left them both hopelessly addicted to the oxytocin produced by being in each other's company. They now spend time searching for vegetation with which to line their starter home, a nest off to the side of a newly-dug burrow. During their off-hours, they spend a good deal of time grooming each other, especially when either has been mistreated – a behavior trait that some scientists consider a sign of animal empathy.

Speaking of grooming, the nearly seven-hour age gap between husband and wife – she was born thirty-eight days ago at 3:07 p.m., while he

trailed her, arriving at 9:59 – might raise a few eyebrows, in a species that possesses eyebrows. But with a lifespan of one year, and hungry great horned owls infesting Chicago, and a certain Lincoln Park homeowner furiously exchanging irate text messages with his gardener, this bonded pair may feel that life is too short to worry about a thing like that.

TWO LUCKY MEMBERS OF THE SMALL-BATCH artisanal antelope species known as "Kirk's dik-dik" (*Madoqua kirkii*) announced their marriage Thursday. How did they make that announcement? Therein lies a tale.

They met that morning when she used the distinctive nasal alarm call that unites the four types of East African antelopes who share the iconic "dik dik" brand to warn him away from a hungry and well-hidden monitor lizard. The distinctive cry of the dik-dik sounds – there is sometimes truth in advertising – like someone yelling *Dik! Dik!* Having heard her message, and noticed her tubular snout, he tried to initiate conversation with a little whistle. But it's hard to land an opening line with a gal who is running in a zigzag pattern at a rate of twenty-six miles per hour.

He caught up with her again a few hours later, though he had to frighten off some rivals before things could get serious. (He rushed forward and nodded his head at them rather markedly.) She liked his three-inch horns – some women appreciate a short king. After that, there weren't too many preliminaries: a lifted foreleg, a bit of smelling.

Then the nuptials began. With him standing behind her, the very model of a supportive modern husband, she left a bit of dung and urine to mark the couple's new territory. He gave the leavings a friendly sniff, bared his teeth, and left a contribution of his own on top. The ceremony was private and attended only by the bride and groom.

Both spouses share a love of solo travel (no packs for the bohemian dik-dik), ruminating, and licking each other's preorbital glands. They are already expecting their first offspring, a boy, who will live at home for seven months, at which point Dad will chase him away. Barring lion attacks, they expect up to a decade of matrimonial bliss.

AN ENTERPRISING PUBLIC-RELATIONS FIRM should take up the cause of the albatross. Contrary to popular belief, sailors do eat them – or at least they did until the Romantic writer, intellectual, and arch anti-albatross propagandist Samuel Taylor Coleridge turned them into an omen of marine doom. A classic Monty Python sketch suggested that they'd taste bad on a stick. (So would the members of Monty Python.) The Japanese call them "fool birds," and the post-punk music group Public Image Ltd named one of the most unpleasant songs in modern history after them. Charles Baudelaire may have delivered the ultimate insult when he compared them to poets.

But they're really not such bad birds. Tourists love them. The Māori make flutes from their bones. In full flight, they look unmistakably cool, with the largest wingspan of any living bird species. And they're loyal, mating more or less for life.

Two majestic Falkland Island black-browed albatrosses have announced the culmination of their lengthy engagement and the beginning of a roughly ten-week incubation period, with bride and groom splitting nest time.

The pair fell in love two years ago, at eight years of age, when they both returned as usual to the rocky outcropping that serves as a winter vacation compound for this highly exclusive extended family. The family that winters together stays together, and older birds in the clan soon noticed this pair practicing the various synchronized grooming, beak-clacking, bowing, and whooping that every albatross pair needs to do to know they're meant to be. When September rolled around again, they danced in unison for hours, and were even heard to moo at each other. For a pair of ten-year-old albatrosses, there's only one thing that can mean.

Once the happy couple's chicks are hatched and fledged, Mom and Dad will return to the long solo flights that form the bread and butter of their daily routine. Barring unforeseen circumstances, they will meet again on that rocky outcropping next September, and for many Septembers after that. They will preen each other's feathers and touch beaks. If the mood strikes, the paterfamilias will sire more eggs.

A contingency that threatens this rosy future is climate change, which researchers have found is driving a spike in the generally low divorce rates among *Thalassarche melanophris*, Falkland Island black-browed albatrosses. Scientists hypothesize that greater than average seasonal differences in sea temperatures make it harder for the birds to know when it's time to return to the family compound for breeding season, and with timetables thus scrambled, homewrecker males have a chance to move in. Warmer oceans also choke the food supply, and as the old saying goes: when poverty comes in at the door, love goes out the window.

Human greed, it seems, is the real albatross. ➤

Tiny Knights

MAUREEN SWINGER

Some life lessons are best taught by King Arthur, Robin Hood, and the occasional cowboy.

THE SMALL SQUIRE grips her shield tighter and starts down the trail, as the trees close overhead. She has prepared herself for the unknown, but not for the path to be quite this gloomy. It doesn't occur to her that she has played in these woods all her life; now she's on a journey, and if she lives up to her code of chivalry, she'll be knighted by the end of this quest. As she passes under each branch, she recites the code: "Be loyal to the King. Fight against evil and hatred. Do not give up in the face of danger. Do not boast. Protect the poor and needy. Give generously to all. Be gentle and courteous to

Maureen Swinger is a senior editor at Plough. *She lives at the Fox Hill Bruderhof in Walden, New York, with her husband, Jason, and their three children.*

ladies. Right what is wrong. Be ready to die for your people." And one more provisional order for this particular quest: "Don't be tempted to stray from the path."

She hoists her shield higher on her shoulder, swings her bag of provisions jauntily, wonders if she's traveled long enough to warrant a bite of the juicy apple that keeps bumping against her leg. She jumps back as a stranger steps from the shadows, stooped, haggard, and – ah! – unarmed. "Good day, sir," she inquires in her bravest voice. "Are you well?" "I am so very hungry," answers the shabbily dressed fellow. "Could you spare me a bite to eat?" "Here, you can have my apple, it's very good," replies the small squire, bestowing her gift with a wobbly smile. She skip-marches down the path, unaware that her lovely apple has met with six others in the stranger's pack, and will be joined by four more by evening's end. He can't afford to enjoy one, even though he is getting rather hungry, because the next squire will be coming down the trail as soon as the last one is out of sight.

Over a small rise, our knight-in-training encounters an old lady whose barrow of rocks has spilled all over the road. The poor woman is so tired, yet she must bring her load home before nightfall. The young squire jumps to the task and soon has the barrow filled, offering to push it where it needs to go. But the grandmother graciously declines, saying she'll manage fine from here, and she waves her thanks till the dauntless young squire reaches the bend in the road, then begins to lift the rocks back out of the cart – at least so it appears to the squire as she

looks back once before turning the bend. But perhaps it was just a trick of the shadows.

Our adventurer is wandering through the prettiest nook in the woods, and perhaps her guard is down, because when a wood nymph with silky lavender locks and a winning grin lilts from a thicket, "Lollipops! Come sample my lovely lollipops!" her front foot is off the path and into the high grass at once. Luckily her back foot lags a little, while her conscience consults the code. No, that nymph is flitting from tree to tree, each one further from the path. Such lollipops are not in the squire's lexicon. Right foot rejoins left on the narrow road to knighthood, and the tempting call of the siren, though suspiciously louder and more incessant now that it has been refused, can be safely ignored.

Victory! At the forest's edge await Arthur and Guinevere, a cohort of fellow squires, and a bevy of knights and ladies – all, as fate would have it, parents of the courageous questers, standing ready with hugs and congratulations. A knighting ceremony ensues, followed by a banquet, jousting tournament, archery, and general merriment.

W ITH THIS INITIATION, my first-grade daughter joins a long line of Bruderhof kids knighted during summer camp – including, once upon a time, myself.

Bruderhof schools keep their doors open in summer, though the kids join the rest of the community for lunch, and take a midday hour to chill at home. Activities range from hiking to gardening, swimming, camping, and nature

The happiest summers of my childhood were spent in Camelot, Sherwood Forest, and along the Oregon Trail.

Opposite: Young squires return victorious from a quest.

study. Some of the older groups might practice and perform an outdoor play. But the younger ages will often theme their summer around a storybook they're reading together, usually one of courage and adventure, be it Robin Hood and his merry men, cowboys of the old West, or knights of the Round Table. Hands down, the happiest summers of my childhood were spent in Camelot, Sherwood Forest, and along the Oregon Trail: wearing green and swinging out of trees, shooting homemade bows and arrows, or slapping on a Stetson and learning to ride an ornery pony. Oh, the wide-open plains of southwest Pennsylvania!

> There will be grand forest adventures, but also stars to earn through the age-old virtues of honor, honesty, valor, and loyalty.

Admittedly, I was a kid with a runaway imagination, and I came by it honestly. My paternal grandfather, John Bazeley, hailed from Merrie Olde England, reveled in tales of Sherwood, and was in fact passionately devoted to the idea of redistributing the ill-gotten gains of the wealthy to those whom they had exploited. In another age, however apocryphal, he might have signed on with Robin's men, though there could have been one hitch; he was also rather proud of the family name, which in its Norman form Basilia dates back to sometime in the 1100s and has a crest which involves such flourishes as: "Azure, three Fleur de Lys Argent, and a Hand holding a Chapeau between Two Branches of Laurel."

My grandmother was, if possible, even more romantic. Perhaps we could blame it on her name: Marguerite Gwladys Dering (I always thought that ought to be prefaced by the word Lady, but she went by Peggy – shortened to Pegs by her sisters Josephine and Yvonne, also known as Jo and Bobs). When she lent me her beloved King Arthur storybook, given to her by her father on her ninth birthday, she told me it was the only possession she had left from her childhood.

When she contracted some dread childhood fever at age ten, all her toys and books were thrown out for fear of contagion. She grabbed this one precious volume off the heap and, in tones as regal as the Lady of the Lake's, declared: "It shall not burn!" Her father did the courtly thing, patiently fumigating every page with a hot poker. In fact, the book was in more danger from the poker than anyone was from possible contagion, but it survived, and so did a good story. I had my turn to pore over the well-worn pages and the forty-eight gorgeous "color plates," clasping the handle of an imaginary sword as it emerged from the waters of a lake and declaring it Excalibur.

A century post-poker, my daughter follows suit. Then she suits up in her knight gear – actually more of a Shieldmaiden-of-Rohan look – and goes questing. Or, likely in future summers, Sherwooding or cattle-herding.

Now, as in my own childhood, neither teachers nor kids make any of these themes a gender-specific thing. "We're cowboys this summer!" is the blissful announcement to parents some June evening, and then girls and boys alike get busy learning the songs, building a chuck wagon, making a prairie camp, figuring out saddles and tack. Or, "We're learning chivalry!" There's going to be a castle somewhere, and our very own shields to make and inscribe. There will be grand forest adventures, but also stars to earn through the age-old virtues of honor, honesty, valor, and loyalty.

Young knights may earn stars around their community by opening doors for the elderly, offering to push someone's wheelchair, or running helpful errands. King Arthur may notice and add a shiny star to a shield, but it may also happen that nobody notices at all, and that star is between the knight and the person she assisted. It's still there.

What is honor? It may be something as humble as not taking the last cookie on the snack plate because a friend also looks hungry. Loyalty comes in many guises, such as walking with the squire who is falling behind on a longer quest. Or rejoicing in the knighthood of Sir Robert who just made it back from the hospital in time for the ceremony, and celebrating what he contributes to the Round Table. And valor too is open to interpretation. It's not only found in daring a path through a dim forest, but in facing up to a fellow knight who's become a bit of a braggart. You might think of courtly dignity in the modern terms of self-respect.

The author's daughter awaits her turn to be knighted.

THESE LESSONS IN CHARACTER are vividly illustrated by the heraldry that each child chooses and paints on her personal shield. My daughter chose a camel and an apple, and while I was delightedly picturing those two items in close proximity, she informed me that in heraldry, a camel represents patience and perseverance, and an apple, happiness and peace. (She also threw in a big red Saint George's Cross for strength.) I was glad my amusement hadn't reached the surface yet, and as she shot out of the room to tell her dad, I thought on the meanings of her first and second names – this surprise child, who does nothing slowly or in half measures. Grace of God and Happy One.

Camels and apples. Perseverance and peace. What did my daughter learn this summer? To shield, help, and uplift. Perhaps next year she'll be herding hypothetical cattle or building a bower in the greenwood. The virtue of such shared imagination is more than reenacting might-have-beens. It's experiencing what could be, a joint lesson in the starting point for all adventures, all beginnings: "I am here on this beautiful earth for some good reason. Others will need my help on the road and I will need theirs. Forward!"

PLOUGH BOOKLIST

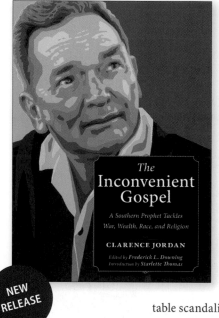

NEW RELEASE

Plough Spiritual Guides

Plough Spiritual Guides briefly introduce the writings of great spiritual voices of the past to new readers. Discover time-tested, life-changing wisdom in these compact, portable books that can be revisited often.

The Inconvenient Gospel
A Southern Prophet Tackles War, Wealth, Race, and Religion
Clarence Jordan

Edited by Frederick L. Downing

On 440 depleted acres in Sumter County, Georgia, a young Baptist preacher and farmer named Clarence Jordan gathered a few families and set out to show that Jesus intended more than spiritual fellowship. Like the first Christians, they would share their land, money, and possessions. Working together to rejuvenate the soil and the local economy, they would demonstrate racial and social justice with their lives.

Black and white community members eating together at the same table scandalized local Christians, drew the ire of the KKK, and led to drive-by shootings, a firebombing, and an economic boycott.

This bold experiment in nonviolence, economic justice, and sustainable agriculture was deeply rooted in Clarence Jordan's understanding of the person and teachings of Jesus, which stood in stark contrast to the hypocrisy of churches that blessed wars, justified wealth disparity, and enforced racial segregation.

This selection from his talks and writings introduces Clarence Jordan's radically biblical vision to a new generation of peacemakers and community builders.

Softcover, 152 pages, ~~$12.00~~, **$8.40 with subscriber discount**

Thunder in the Soul
To Be Known by God
Abraham Joshua Heschel

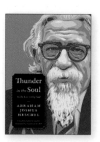

Edited by Robert Erlewine

Foreword by Susannah Heschel

Like the Hebrew prophets before him, the great American rabbi and civil rights leader reveals God's concern for this world and each of us.

Softcover, 168 pages, ~~$12.00~~, **$8.40 with subscriber discount**

Love in the Void
Where God Finds Us

Simone Weil

Simone Weil, with her short, troubled life and confounding insights into faith and doubt, continues to speak to today's spiritual seekers.

Softcover, 134 pages, ~~$12.00~~, **$8.40 with subscriber discount**

That Way and No Other
Following God through Storm and Drought

Amy Carmichael

How do you stay true to God's call for your life? Amy Carmichael left everything to become a missionary in India, but then a child fleeing sexual slavery gave her a new vocation.

Softcover, 144 pages, ~~$12.00~~, **$8.40 with subscriber discount**

The Reckless Way of Love
Notes on Following Jesus

Dorothy Day

How do you follow Jesus without burning out? Dorothy Day offers hard-earned wisdom and practical advice gained through decades of seeking to know Jesus and to follow his example.

Softcover, 149 pages, ~~$12.00~~, **$8.40 with subscriber discount**

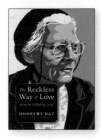

The Scandal of Redemption
When God Liberates the Poor, Saves Sinners, and Heals Nations

Oscar Romero

"A church that does not provoke crisis, a gospel that does not disturb, a word of God that does not touch the concrete sin of the society in which it is being proclaimed – what kind of gospel is that?"

Softcover, 139 pages, ~~$12.00~~, **$8.40 with subscriber discount**

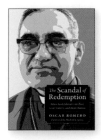

The Prayer God Answers

Eberhard Arnold and Richard J. Foster

Eberhard Arnold describes the kind of prayer that pleases God – prayer that has the power to transform our lives and our world.

Softcover, 80 pages, ~~$8.00~~, **$5.60 with subscriber discount**

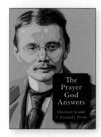

Forgiveness

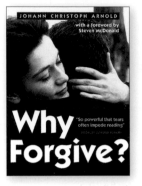

Why Forgive?

Johann Christoph Arnold

In *Why Forgive?* Arnold lets people speak for themselves – people who have earned the right to talk about overcoming hurt, and about the peace of mind they have found in doing so. Translated into more than twenty languages, this modest but compelling volume of true stories has been reprinted hundreds of times, and sold or distributed to audiences around the world.

Nelson Mandela: A much-needed message not only for South Africa, but for the whole world.

Booklist (starred review): A most impressive book . . . so powerful that tears often impede reading.

Softcover, 232 pages, $12.00, **$8.40 with subscriber discount**

You Carried Me

A Daughter's Memoir

Melissa Ohden

Melissa Ohden is fourteen when she learns that she is the survivor of a botched abortion. In *You Carried Me*, she details her search for her biological parents and her own journey from anger and shame to faith and forgiveness.

Kirkus Reviews: A memoir of mothers, daughters, adoption, and abortion. . . . Ohden's story is complicated, and she has impressively overcome significant emotional challenges. . . . [Her] perseverance is inspiring.

Softcover, 200 pages, $15.99, **$11.19 with subscriber discount**

From Red Earth

A Rwandan Story of Healing and Forgiveness

Denise Uwimana

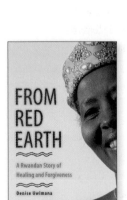

Denise Uwimana gave birth to her third son at the height of the Rwandan genocide. With the unlikely help of Hutu Good Samaritans, she and her children survived. Her husband and other family members were not as lucky. The stories she has uncovered through her work and recounted here illustrate the complex and unfinished work of truth-telling, recovery, and reconciliation that may be Rwanda's lasting legacy.

Booklist: Rwandan genocide survivor Denise Uwimana recounts in painful detail the bloody tragedy of her country. . . . She moves forward to explain how forgiveness has become crucial in her life and the lives of others. Gut-wrenching but undeniably compelling, this is a powerful look at Rwanda, then and now.

Softcover, 232 pages, $18.00, **$12.60 with subscriber discount**

(continued from p. 120)

Instead, on the day of his baptism, he vanished into the mountains. He reappeared a month later, wearing a saffron robe, looking like any one of the Hindu sadhus or Buddhist lamas who traversed the country.

Having made his baptismal vows, he made other commitments: he would be celibate. He would travel. And he would do this as an Indian holy man, not as an agent of colonial power. "I am not worthy to follow in the steps of my Lord," he said, "but, like him, I want no home, no possessions. Like him I will belong to the road, sharing the suffering of my people, eating with those who will give me shelter, and telling all people of the love of God."

Tales of healings and visions cluster around these years. He worked for a time in a leper colony. And there were many conversions. Everywhere he went, he spoke of the Christ who was both the Way and the destination of that Way, the Christ who was the end of every pilgrimage and the light of every enlightenment.

Christianity was not a faith foreign to India. The apostle Thomas is said to have traveled there; the Indian Orthodox Church is two thousand years old. But Sundar felt himself to be the heir of his mother's spiritual quest, which had led through Hindu, Buddhist, and Sikh traditions.

It was to the seekers that he went. And he went where they went: into the mountains, toward Tibet, pressing to the roof of the world.

He recalled a conversation he had had, during these travels, with an old lama who lived in a cave. The two exchanged notes on their spiritual paths. "What have you gained through your seclusion and meditation?" Sundar asked.

"I seek nirvana, the elimination of all feeling and all desire – whether of pain or of peace. But still I live in spiritual darkness. I do not know what the end will be."

Sadhu Sundar Singh

"Surely, your longings and feelings arise from the God who created you," Sundar responded. "They were surely created in order to be fulfilled, not crushed. The destruction of all desire cannot lead to release, but only to suicide. Are not our desires inseparably intertwined with the continuation of life? . . . Surely we shall find peace not by eliminating desire, but by finding its fulfillment and satisfaction in the One who created it."

After World War I, he visited Ceylon, Burma, China, Japan, Britain, the United States, and Europe. He was appalled by the West – the Lost Generation with its grasping after immediate pleasure. It seemed empty to him: India, he thought, had at the very least a sense of the divine.

The traveling took its toll. By 1923, his health failing, he settled down to write and live the life of Christian fellowship. By this time, he had reconciled with his father, who had himself converted.

But in 1929, the road called again. The last trace of him that we have is word of his leaving a town in the foothills of the Himalayas, heading into the mountains, in the company of other pilgrims. He was never seen again.

Sundar's writings have come to be appreciated by Orthodox, Catholic, and Protestant Christians the world over. Even the Anglican Church has given him a feast day, June 19. I suspect Sundar would have something to say about that. To be commemorated posthumously by the Western Christianity that he so vigorously critiqued is a plot twist that would probably make him smile. ➳

Sadhu Sundar Singh

A modern Saint Francis, Sundar Singh left his family and ancestral faith to follow Jesus without Western trappings.

SUSANNAH BLACK ROBERTS

Opposite: Ned Gannon, Sadhu Sundar Singh, 2022

1903, PUNJAB, INDIA. The fourteen-year-old boy wakes up at three in the morning, bathes, and chants the Sikh morning prayer:

> One universal creator God. His name is Truth. Creative being personified. . . . Image of the Undying, beyond birth, self-existent. . . . How can you become truthful? And how can the veil of illusion be torn away?

His mother had taught him the prayers: she had been, he said, "a living example of the love of God." And now she was dead.

Three days before, at school, he had horrified his father by burning a Bible. He was full of frustration and rage: the gurus his mother had taken him to meet had themselves been hunters after God, seekers of the peace he himself craved. And this Christianity was the religion of the colonizers.

"I prayed," he wrote later of that moment, "that if there was a God at all, he would reveal himself to me. Should I receive no answer by morning, I would place my head on the railroad tracks and seek the answer to my questions beyond the edge of this life."

An hour and a half later, he saw something like a glow in the room. And then he saw someone in the light. That someone spoke, in Urdu.

"Sundar, how long will you mock me? I have come to save you because you have prayed to find the way of truth. Why then don't you accept it?"

It was then I saw the marks of blood on his hands and feet and knew that it was Yesu, the one proclaimed by the Christians. In amazement I fell at his feet. I was filled with deep sorrow and remorse for my insults and my irreverence, but also with a wonderful peace. This was the joy I had been seeking.

He immediately went to tell his father that he was going to be a follower of Jesus now. His father told him to go back to sleep.

In the morning, though, Sundar didn't budge, despite his father's pleadings: he was going to be baptized. He cut off his hair, the long hair that is the mark of a Sikh man. His father, grief-stricken, spoke a vow: "We reject you forever and cast you from among us. You shall be no more my son. . . . For us, you are as one who was never born."

Sundar explained himself to the missionaries at his school – the ones he had mocked. They sent him to a nearby boarding school. On his sixteenth birthday, in the parish church in Shimla, at the foothills of the Himalayas, he was baptized.

He might have become an Anglican minister, or a state administrator, rising up the ranks in the massive colonial apparatus.

(continued on previous page)

Susannah Black Roberts is a senior editor at Plough. *She lives in New York City.*